P9-BIB-070

They had it made.

The sixteen athletes in this book kicked, skied, skated, vaulted and dribbled their way to the top in the sports world—winners all.

Like Paul Henderson—Toronto Maple Leafs forward who scored ''the goal of the century'' in the first Canada-Russia series.

Or Jennifer Diachun Palmer—Canadian Olympic gymnast and 1974 National Champion.

Or placekicker Gerry Organ—Schenley award winner, four-time Eastern Football Conference scoring champ with over 1,000 career points, and 1972's Most Valuable Player.

Fame, success, awards, money...they got their share and more.

But it wasn't enough.

FREE AGENTS

FREE AGENTS

by
Jim Talentino

Horizon House Publishers
Box 600
Beaverlodge, Alberta, Canada

To my wife, Cyndi,
who throughout the process of writing has sacrificed,
thought, worked and prayed for its successful
completion. Her guidance is appreciated.

Contents

Acknowledgements

I would never have written this book except for the imprint of many people on my life. Through the efforts of Aunt Jessie's prayers in Nanaimo, B.C., the witness of Zig Ziglar in New Orleans, Louisiana, and the teaching of Everett Barnard in Indianapolis, Indiana, I was introduced to the Lord Jesus Christ in February, 1979.

Many have guided my spiritual growth with their writings and insights into Scripture. Rev. Lloyd Patterson, Rev. Gene Kimble, the late Rev. A.W. Tozer, Rev. John Stott, Rev. J.V. Dahms, Dr. Stan Willson, Rev. Sam Stoesz, Dr. Francis Schaeffer, and Rev. T.V. Thomas have been valuable sources of spiritual input.

Gratitude is extended to Canadian Theological College for allowing me to study and broaden my awareness and understanding of the Christian life.

Sincere affection is extended to my home church, Hope, and to Duane Ranard and May Moody for being such an encouragement.

Special mention is due my family. Terry, my father,

who has spent his life in athletics and also Patti, Shannon and Mary Lynn.

All the above helped to prepare me to write **Free Agents**, which was made possible by Athletes in Action, Campus Crusade for Christ, and Teen Ranch. May they be blessed for their faith and ministry.

Introduction

This book has come into being through the cooperative efforts of two Canadian organizations—Athletes in Action—Canada and Teen Ranch, Caledon, Ontario.

Athletes in Action (AIA), a ministry of Campus Crusade for Christ with Canadian headquarters in Abbotsford, B.C., exists for two purposes: to win athletes to Christ, teaching them how to live an abundant Christian life; and to provide Christian athletes with opportunities to share their faith with other athletes and with the general population.

To accomplish these purposes, AIA sponsors pre-game chapels, team meetings, Bible studies and conferences.

An exciting development occurred in 1978-79 when AIA launched the Athletes in Action—Canada basketball team. Striving to be the top amateur team in the world and using their athletic abilities as an opportunity to share the life-changing message of Jesus Christ are priorities. A highlight was their victory over the second-ranked team in the world—the Soviet Union National Team.

Teen Ranch, located at Caledon, Ontario, is a

year-round horsemanship camp founded in 1967 by Mel Stevens and his wife, Janet. Attracting young people to the gospel through sports activities, the ranch has since expanded its program to include English riding, hockey camp, tennis camp, and rugger camp. Facilities are also available for year-round retreats for student and church groups.

Christian professional athletes volunteer their services regularly to minister to young people at Teen Ranch. As well, Mel Stevens is chaplain to the Toronto Argonauts, conducts Bible studies and chapels for the Toronto Maple Leafs, and has a similar involvement with several Junior A hockey teams. In cooperation with Athletes in Action, Mel is also a regular speaker at chapels for professional baseball and football teams from all across Canada.

FREE AGENTS was initiated primarily through the individual efforts of Mel Stevens of Teen Ranch, and Gordon Barwell, former Saskatchewan Roughrider and Toronto-based Regional Director of Athletes in Action. Bob Kraemer, former Winnipeg Blue Bomber, provides national leadership for AIA, and Marvin Kehler is national director of Campus Crusade for Christ.

1

The Goal of the Century
Paul Henderson

Like thousands of other young boys playing minor hockey across Canada, he had dreamed of playing professional. While playing in a juvenile game at age 16 in his hometown of Lucknow, Ontario, he proceeded to score 18 goals in one game. Hockey scouts took note. They figured that young Paul Henderson had the stamp of a future pro. Little did anyone realize at the time that he was to score the most famous and emotional goal of the century!

Paul played his Junior hockey under legendary coach Eddie Bush and the Hamilton Red Wings. He benefited greatly from the daily practice sessions and the intense competition in the league. He began to polish his natural talents and skills.

"I would work on the areas that I couldn't do well. I worked hard at getting the puck away quicker. The less time a goalie has to prepare for a shot, the greater advantage the shooter has. A quick release became my biggest asset as a hockey player," remembers Paul.

"Eddie would always tell us, 'You've got a whole career to win the Stanley Cup, but you've only got a couple of years for a crack at the Memorial Cup.' ''

Symbolic of Canadian Junior Hockey supremacy, the Memorial Cup came to the Hamilton Red Wings in Paul's final year. Paul had an excellent individual year as well. He led the league with 49 goals, and turned professional with Detroit of the NHL.

The nervous and excited young rookie received no special consideration in his first game. ''Dickie Duff of the Leafs welcomed me to the league on my first shift,'' Paul remembers. ''He gave me a good going over in front of the Leaf net and the referee gave me seven minutes in penalties.'' The future hero had made his pro debut.

Paul spent five years with Detroit until he was involved in a sensational trade with the Toronto Maple Leafs. Punch Imlach had grown dissatisfied with the great Frank Mahovlich and shipped him, Garry Unger, Peter Stemkowski and Carl Brewer to Detroit. In return, the Leafs received Henderson, Norm Ullman, and Floyd Smith. It was March 1968, and Paul was upset: ''At the time I was really disappointed. I loved playing in Detroit and hated to leave.''

But there were bigger and better things in store for Paul Henderson.

It was while he was with Toronto that he was selected to play for Team Canada in 1972. The confrontation was a classic from the outset. The Russians had dominated European hockey for years. Canada had not been represented in the World Championships for some time as there were NHL schedule conflicts. As well, Canada's best players were professionals in the NHL and therefore ineligible for international competition. An

16

exhibition series was proposed, meeting their challenge, to decide true hockey supremacy.

The date was set for September 1972, thus avoiding any NHL schedule problems. The series was regarded as a joke by most Canadians. Proud of their hockey heritage and convinced of their superiority, they paid no heed to warnings from the late Lloyd Percival, whose coaching principles the Russians followed with zeal. Most of the Team Canada players felt relaxed as they read advance scouting reports from Bob Davidson and the late Johnny McClellan of the Leafs. After a quick trip to Europe, the scouts returned saying the Russian goalie wouldn't have a chance against NHL shooters. It was a prediction they would never be able to live down.

After the long previous season, most of the NHL players relaxed during the summer by playing golf and lounging. On another continent, the Russians were intense and zealous in their preparations. Every minute, every drill, every drop of sweat was spent to defeat Team Canada. They knew what was at stake and they wanted it badly—world hockey supremacy. They had played and trained as a unit for months; they were like a machine!

Canadians smiled and scoffed at their ridiculous practice sessions, their funny-looking equipment, their language, and their customs. But most foolishly, they laughed and dismissed as ridiculous the Russian dream of defeating Team Canada.

So it was that the series opened in Montreal. It was to be an eight-game series, with the first four games in four different Canadian cities across the country. The last four games were to be played in Moscow. Canadians predicted a total sweep for the NHL; the

Russians would be lucky to emerge with their pride intact. The publicity build-up had reached the peak of hype and emotions soared equally as high. Was there a television set in Canada that did not broadcast the excited voice of the Montreal Canadiens' Danny Gallivan, booming out the odd-sounding Russian names?

Opening ceremonies at the Montreal Forum included the Canadian Prime Minister, Pierre Trudeau, and various political dignitaries from both countries. As the national anthems of both countries were played, it seemed as if the roof of the Forum could not contain the excitement, tension and emotion within its walls. The series had begun as a hockey game between two teams. It was now much more than that. Patriotic pride filled everyone who witnessed the event. It was now country against country. It was Canada versus Russia! It was war on ice!

Team Canada exploded from the drop of the puck. Before Danny Gallivan had a chance to get settled, they put the puck past the Russian goalie. The country breathed a sigh of relief and settled in for the humiliation of this Russian team that had the audacity to challenge the best of the NHL.

But the game was far from over. The Russians had not yet begun. They stunned the hockey world by soundly defeating Team Canada 7-3 in the opening game. Tretiak, the Russian goalie, who had been considered a pushover, was a household name across Canada by the next morning. He had closed the door on the world's top shooters. The reaction was like a tidal wave.

Fans who for years had been told of the superiority of the NHL game and had paid higher ticket prices without question were astonished. They hated to see Team Canada lose, but the Russian style of play was beautiful to watch. It was refreshing; it was smooth; they were master fundamentalists.

Team Canada players and coaches were embarrassed, frustrated, angry. They were outplayed and could not keep up with the superbly conditioned Soviet athletes. They could not understand the criticism levelled at them by the media and people across the country. They had been booed and berated. Their bodies bore bruises and welts from the vicious stick work of the Soviet players. They had given up their holidays to play for their country and felt they weren't being appreciated. Perhaps the biggest blow was to their professional pride and egos. They had assumed they were the finest in the world, and they had been proven wrong.

The situation worsened and tension increased as the series progressed across the country. The Soviets were no longer hockey players—they were Communists. After the final game in Canada, in Vancouver, the series score told a grim tale: of a possible and expected eight points, Team Canada had gained only three—one win and a tie in four games. Despair set in and gloomy predictions were made as the distraught team headed for the bigger Russian ice surface in Moscow. It would enable the Soviets to free-wheel in their systematic style, and would put the Canadians at an even greater disadvantage with their inferior conditioning.

One line was seeing a lot of action in the series. It was made up of Paul Henderson, Ron Ellis of the Leafs, and Bobby Clarke of the Philadelphia Flyers.

The fifth game exposed Canadians to the unfamiliar

setting of the Moscow Ice Stadium. Papers were full of stories of the difficulties the players and the rest of the Canadian contingent were facing. Poor hotel accommodations, strange food, and the constant and highly visible military presence—all bore heavily on everyone's mind. Constant whistling from the crowd, a European form of booing, shrieked through the stadium. Leonid Brezhnev, President of the Soviet Union, was in attendance. Nationalistic pride in the hearts of both Russians and Canadians had reached a feverish pitch.

Team Canada replied with everything they had, and went into the dressing room at the end of the second period leading 4-2. There was a new spirit in the dressing room; finally things were turning around; they began to relax. Coaches go sleepless and turn grey when this attitude of complacency settles in a dressing room—"Roses are red; violets are blue. We've got four and they've got two."

"We should have won that game," remembers Ron Ellis, "but they turned it around in the third period and beat us."

The Russians had refused to quit, and now the same test would be put to the Canadians. They now had their backs to the wall. In order to win the series, they had to win the last three games in Moscow.

Paul Henderson was ready. "The pressure was unbelievable; each day it just grew and grew. We slept, ate and talked hockey. A lot of people had already counted us out, but we were still confident we could do it."

Both teams were fully aware of the importance of the game. The checking was tight, resulting in a scoreless first period. The Russians came out eager to score that precious first goal early in the second period, and did so with only 1:12 gone on the clock. The psychological edge shifted and Canadian fans stirred uncomfortably.

Suddenly Team Canada exploded with an outstanding offensive display of three goals in only one minute twenty-three seconds. Dennis Hull and Yvan Cournoyer scored the first two, with Paul Henderson scoring the third and eventual game winner. The Russians fought back with their second goal near the end of the second period, but the third period remained scoreless. From the brink of defeat the Canadians were given new hope. It was a hope that surged across the country as they rested for game seven.

Game seven was no different. It was tension-packed and, with less than three minutes remaining in the third period, the Canadians were once again frustrated. They had again played well enough to win, but until this point could only manage a tie. They had to win—a tie was not sufficient and would make the eighth game meaningless. Paul Henderson was on the ice, with both teams playing a man short.

"Serge Savard hit me with a pass on our side of the red line and I went in on their two defensemen," recalls Paul. "I went to the outside, slipping the puck between the defenseman's legs. I had him beat on the outside and was cutting for the net when the defenseman tripped me and I fell to the ice. I got my shot off though."

The quick shot went over the Russian goalie Tretiak's shoulder before Paul hit the ice. The Russians were stunned and Team Canada went wild. Tretiak and Henderson were having their own private battle, with Tretiak losing the first two rounds.

But the crucial test still lay ahead. The whole series now boiled down to one game. With all their efforts and heroics, the Canadians had but gained equal footing with the Russians. Both teams were now under the same pressure for the first time since the opening face-off in Montreal.

Was there anyone in Canada who was not caught up in the emotion leading up to the eighth and final game? The Moscow Stadium was like a circus. It was an almost impossible dream; could the Canadians do it? It didn't appear so to anyone on the outside looking in. After two periods of play, Team Canada was down 5-3.

Linemate Ron Ellis reflects back on what went on in the Canadian dressing room: "We were really very confident even though we were two goals down. We were very high and in good spirits. We were outplaying them and our game was finally coming together. Some of the guys gave 'Henny' a shot about pulling it out of the fire again."

Another twenty minutes and it would be all over. So the Canadians fought back with everything they had. But it wasn't enough; with 45 seconds remaining they were tied 5-5 and again it wasn't good enough. They had to win.

"Our line was on the bench, and a fresh line was on the ice, so I was really surprised when I saw Peter coming off and Paul going over the boards," remembers Ellis.

Paul Henderson recalls, "I just had a feeling I could score the winner. I yelled at Peter Mahovlich to come off and hopped the boards. As I hit the ice, Brad Park had the puck at the point in their end. I raced for the net and yelled at him. He tried to hit me with the pass, but it was behind me and a Russian defenseman took me out. Because I was going so fast, I crashed into the end boards behind the net. Millions reacted in frustration; it was too late; it was all over. While I was getting up I saw that Phil Esposito and Yvon Cournoyer were putting real pressure on their defenseman who was trying to clear the puck out of the Russian end. Then the Russian made a very uncharacteristic bad pass. Phil intercepted the pass and I yelled at him as I headed to the front of the net.''

The man who had worked so hard on his quick release years ago took the pass and snapped his wrists. The Soviet goalie blocked the shot but couldn't control the rebound. Paul quickly put the loose puck behind Tretiak.

The Russians had been beaten with 34 seconds left on the clock. Canadians all over the world exploded with emotion. People across Canada jumped into their cars and started beeping their horns. They marched in the streets with Canadian flags.

''When I saw it hit the net, I went completely bonkers,'' remembers Paul. ''I immediately wished my dad was there to see it—he died in 1968. I was totally consumed by the whole thing. I was emotionally and physically drained. It was over; what a sense of relief. I just wanted to get out of Moscow as quickly as I could. We landed in Montreal and Toronto and the reception we got was beyond anything I could ever have imagined.''

Paul was an instant national hero. Everybody wanted to interview him, and the whole country talked about him. The long NHL season was a grind after what he had been through. His play was affected.

''I used to be a real high-strung individual,'' relates

Paul. "How I felt was based on how I played. If I had a good night, I shot higher than a kite. If we lost, it was an automatic downer. There was no way to keep from going down—I had nothing stable or solid to hang onto."

Bitter contract talks followed with Maple Leaf owner Harold Ballard. The relationship between the two had never been amicable.

"With the Team Canada experience, I had a lot of leverage and I wanted revenge. I was full of bad feelings for the man because of some of our dealings in the past," states Paul. "I was out for all I could get. I am not proud of the way I handled myself during the negotiations.

"I was 29 years old and I'd accomplished everything I'd set out to do as a professional. I had a great wife and three super daughters. I was financially secure; I had essentially everything a man could ask for. Yet, I was not content."

While on a holiday in Switzerland, Paul relaxed in the Alps and thought about his future, and his emptiness. "I decided that if there was a God, I would find him because I needed Him in my life."

Mel Stevens of Teen Ranch in Caledon, Ontario, had recently presented the Leafs with Bibles. Paul became friends with Mel more out of curiosity than anything else.

"He had none of the material things, the worldly prestige or financial security that I had," remembers Paul. "But he really seemed to have a handle on life, and I realized that the concept of God was very real to Mel.

"I really had a lot of questions about different religions and the Bible. Mel and I would study together and over the months I bounced a lot of things off him. I really had four big hang-ups at the time. First, I had to be convinced that I would not have to throw my brains in the garbage can to become a Christian. Second, I was afraid of what my friends would think about me; I didn't want to be known as a religious fanatic. Third, I looked at Christianity as a lot of dos and don'ts and I was reluctant to give up some of my enjoyments. Last, I wasn't too happy about having to stand up and be counted—to declare myself a Christian; I didn't mind talking to Mel or my wife, Eleanor, but as far as anybody else, I just did not feel courageous enough at the time.''

Time passed and Paul, unable to settle his contract problems with the Leafs, jumped leagues and joined the World Hockey Association Toros. One of his new teammates was Frank Mahovlich, who was on the opposite end of the trade years ago that took Paul from Detroit. His internal turmoil continued. Past the halfway mark of the season, he was sidelined with a hip to heel cast. He had injured his knee. Hindered by the cast and by the weather, he spent a lot of time reading at home.

"After days of reading the Bible, I was convinced I wouldn't have to commit intellectual suicide, but I still had all those other hang-ups. I was a frightened young man. Finally one day in the privacy of my den, I asked the Lord Jesus Christ to forgive my sin. I acknowledged my fear and asked Him to change me and strengthen me, as I knew I wasn't going to be able to do it alone. I don't know what I was expecting," he laughs, "maybe bells or flashing lights or who knows what. All there was was the quiet of the room. A peace overwhelmed me; I knew my struggle was over.''

The Toros eventually moved to Birmingham, Alabama, where Paul, wife Eleanor, and three daughters, Heather, Jennifer, and Jill make their home. He was called up to play part of the 79-80 season with the Atlanta Flames, but chose to remain with the minor league team in Birmingham. He is an assistant coach to John Brophy as well, and is uncertain of his future now that the Flames have moved to Calgary.

"I want to remain in the game," says Paul. "It gives me the opportunity to relate to fellow pros and share my faith with them. Hey, I had it all, everything they hope to do, and it wasn't enough for me. I know deep inside other players are not satisfied either. As they search, I can tell them about the Lord Jesus Christ whom I've found."

Of the tens of thousands of young boys who hope, he was one boy who made it. Is there a young boy in the country who doesn't dream of playing in Make Believe Gardens?

"It would be nice for everyone to experience the thrill of playing for the Leafs," says Paul. "It was certainly a thrill for me, but it was also the most disturbing part of my life—the pain, the frustration, the tension that was involved in my contract battles with Harold Ballard. But now I love Harold Ballard and I pray for him. I don't know of any more valuable news that I can give him, than the good news of Christ!"

I denied myself nothing my eyes desired; I refused my heart no pleasure. My heart took delight in all my work, and this was the reward for all my labor. Yet when I surveyed all that my hands had done and what I had toiled to achieve everything was meaningless, a chase after the wind; nothing was gained under the sun. Ecclesiastes 2:10,11

2

Dial Z for Zenon!
Zenon Andrusyshyn

The young Canadian athlete was a long way from his Oakville, Ontario, home. He walked onto the practice field feeling cocky and arrogant. Twenty universities had sought him out, but he had chosen the University of California at Los Angeles. Having represented Canada in the Commonwealth games, he was now preparing for the 1968 Olympic games in Mexico City in his specialty event—the javelin. He smiled to himself as he remembered the first time he had competed in high school; there were six competitors and he finished sixth. But all that had changed now. Here he was—a freshman athlete at one of the greatest athletic campuses in the world.

Impatient, he scoffed at the warm-up exercises and simply went through the motions. Though often considered a waste of time, stretching increases the blood flow to a muscle and increases flexibility and strength. "I'm in great shape," thought the confident young athlete. He remembered how he had trained three hours a day, lifting weights and soaring from 165 lbs. to 196 lbs. in only three months as a 16-year-old.

His mind wandered as the others diligently warmed

up. Finally, he was able to grab a javelin. He loved to watch it arc against the sky in flight. Completing his approach, he thrust the javelin skyward with all his strength and body weight behind it. In that split instant, his elbow snapped. The unstretched muscles could not stand the force.

Surgery proved unsuccessful. Zenon Andrusyshyn's outstanding young career as a track and field athlete was finished; he would never throw the javelin again!

He was disappointed and bitter—all his hopes and dreams had been shattered. For years he had been identified as an athlete; now he was just another campus freshman. He didn't like it and neither did his coaches and the athletic department who had blown a $20,000 investment in him as an athlete. With no goal in sight, he began to drift.

"I didn't know what I was going to do with my life," remembers Zee. "I was pretty bitter about my injury. I had worked hard to become successful. My father had always wanted me to be a good athlete and had encouraged me to play soccer when I was a kid. He had instilled a love for sports in me. I used to play soccer two or three times a week for years before switching to track and field."

The roots of adversity in the Andrusyshyn family ran deep. Although Zee was born in Gunzburg, Germany, his parents were full-blooded Ukrainians. They were forced to go to Germany in the late 1930s and were post-war immigrants to Canada. Thankful for their new-found freedom and opportunity, Zee's parents worked hard to master their new language and to acquire sufficient skills to provide for a new life in Canada.

"One of the major reasons I chose UCLA over all

the other schools was that it symbolized a good time,'' reflects Zee. ''Leaving Toronto International Airport, my mind was racing at 100 miles an hour. All I could think of on the plane was to get to Los Angeles and have a good time; to be on my own, away from my parents. To me UCLA was beaches, girls and music.''

After his injury, Zee pursued his interests fully. ''For about four months, all I did was party and do alcohol and drugs. I was pretty depressed and just couldn't accept what had happened to me.''

Scholarship athletes are given part-time jobs by the Athletic Department to provide for spending money, room and board, or other incidentals. Zee had three responsibilities: sweeping the tunnels under the stadium, turning the sprinklers on and off, and being an usher in Los Angeles Coliseum.

''I used to work up in the 82nd row for the football games,'' states Zee. ''The more football I watched, especially their kickers, the more I realized that I could do just as good a job or better.''

The UCLA Bruins are one of the most successful college football teams in the U.S. It was one thing to be an athlete at UCLA, but it was another step in status to belong to either the football or basketball teams. They had tradition; they had color; they were winners. Although he was only another face in the crowd of 95,000 people who attended the games, the young Canadian began to dream again.

Thousands of dollars and hours are spent recruiting and screening college football players. UCLA and Head Coach Tommy Prothro could afford to be choosy. Only the best need apply. During spring practice, Prothro and his staff were putting their charges through conditioning drills and working on fundamentals in preparation for the upcoming season, when the arrogant and cocky Andrusyshyn of old walked out onto the practice field.

"When I told them I wanted to be their kicker, they were sarcastic and just laughed," states Zee. "They laughed at my name, my attitude, my background... everything about me. I persisted though, and they said they would give me a try-out at the next day's practice."

The coaches were surprised that he even showed up. But they let him show what he could do. By the end of the practice, the UCLA Bruins had a new kicker. Skeptical coaches were now excited coaches. Zee had a new sport—from the 82nd row of the Los Angeles Coliseum to the middle of the action. No more hurling javelins; his business was now booming footballs into the sky.

"I remember our first game; it was against the University of Tennessee. I played a good game in front of the home fans and also a national television audience. I made eight points with two field goals and two converts and we won the game 21-16. I became an instant celebrity."

Zee's life now took on a new dimension. He was a star athlete; he was in the spotlight of a sports and celebrity-mad campus and city. People were enthralled with his unique background and circumstances. He had pulled off the ultimate fantasy. Success after success piled up as the Bruins, week by week, fought their way to the top of the standings. It would all be decided in the last game of the season—a classic showdown for the National Championship. The winner received an automatic berth in the highly prized Rose Bowl. Their opponents—arch rivals, the University of

Southern California.

The tension and excitement continued to build the week before the game. Fans, media, alumni of each school, coaches, and players—all were caught up in the guessing game as to who would come out on top.

"It was some game," recalls Zee, "close all the way. USC had a runningback by the name of O.J. Simpson who had a pretty fair day. I had a couple of field goal attempts blocked. With seven minutes remaining and the score tied 14-14, we made a touchdown. But I missed the convert; the score was 20-14.

"With one minute left, USC made a touchdown. They kicked the extra point and won the game 21-20."

The Bruins had lost their bid for a national championship by one point—a point Zee should have made.

"I felt bad—I had blown it; but I could never imagine how important it was."

Any athlete would love to make the front page of a major city newspaper. It has to be an extraordinary event to go from the sports page to the front page. The early morning edition of the **Los Angeles Times** carried a front page picture of Andrusyshyn sitting all alone at the end of the Bruin's bench. In a year full of the horrors of Vietnam, student riots, racial unrest and political turmoil, the headline screamed, **"DIAL Z FOR ZERO!"**

Zee was hurt and bitter. He began to treat people the same way they treated him. He became a troubled man and a problem athlete. Over the next two years, he used anyone and anything the way he had felt used.

"I hustled the school; I hustled girls; I hustled

people. I did what I wanted and didn't care who got hurt in the process."

The coaches put up with his antics; he was still one of the best kickers in the country. He was nicknamed the "Golden Toe" by the media. After reading the newspapers, Zee walked into Head Coach Prothro's office and told him he wanted his kicking shoe painted gold.

In an age when coaches promoted discipline and conformity, Zee partied the nights away. In an age of short hair, Zee wore long hair and sunglasses.

"I didn't care what they said about me, as long as they were talking about me," states Zee.

He became a two-time All-American and he was expected to go high in the NFL pro draft.

But football coaches are a close family, and word got around about his behavior. He wasn't selected until the 9th round by the Dallas Cowboys. After five games the Cowboys grew tired of his antics and cut him from the roster. He returned to UCLA to complete his degree and while there met Susan Johnson.

"We were perfect for each other: I used her and she used me," says Zee.

Invited to a try-out with the Toronto Argonauts, Zee moved back to Canada and eventually signed with the Argos.

"I asked Susan to come up and live with me, and she did. It was disgraceful to my parents, but I didn't care. I had become numb to other people's feelings. I would argue with my mother and tell her I didn't believe in her God. Everything that people believed about God seemed to be predicated on fear. I refused to be intimidated like that; God didn't exist as far as I was concerned."

Over the next five years, Zee pursued his career with the Argos and his love-hate relationship with Susan. They would live together for awhile until tempers flared and she moved out. They treated each other with total disregard.

The great majority of relationships between pro athletes are superficial. They know their world is a temporary one. Anyone could be missing from the dressing room from one day to the next. As well, in a world where strength and ego are important, one does not want to reveal that he has problems; it is a sign of weakness. Zee found, though, that he could confide in Peter Muller, an Argo teammate, about his problems with his life and Susan.

"I even started going to pre-game chapels," says Zee. "Maybe I was out all night, but I'd put on the sunglasses and turn up for chapel. I trusted Peter and respected him as a friend. He wouldn't preach at me; he was just there whenever I needed him.

"About that time, in 1974, after the season ended, I won the Pro Football Countdown for the Kicker of the Year Award. I flew to Vancouver to pick up the cash and called Susan in Los Angeles.

" 'Sue, will you go to Hawaii with me? I want to marry you.'

" 'Let's not talk about marriage,' she said, 'but I'll go to Hawaii.' "

Three weeks later Sue and Zee were married in Hawaii. On their way back to Toronto, Zee remembered that Peter had invited him to an Athletes In Action Conference in Winnipeg. He had even offered to pay Zee's air fare.

"Sue always liked being around football players, and she liked the part about saving a thousand bucks in air fare, so we went," Zee recalls. "We figured if anyone came up and told us 'You have to accept Jesus,' we'd just pack up and leave.''

After years of bitterness and hate and deceit, they were not prepared for their experience at the Conference.

"We both realized that these people really loved us; they accepted us. I had made a miserable mess of my life, and being newly married, I felt I wanted to start all over again. I hadn't trusted anyone in a long time, but I decided to trust in Jesus Christ. When I got back to the hotel room, I was going to tell Sue, when she told me that she, too, had asked Jesus Christ to forgive her and come into her life."

Growth and enthusiasm were spontaneous. Joyously thankful for Christ's love and forgiveness, they were, in Zee's words, "so fired up for the Lord, we couldn't see straight." Since that time they have hosted Bible studies in their home for other athletes. They took Bible correspondence courses and travelled to South America as missionaries. Both the CFL/NFL veteran and his wife are thankful for the love of Jesus Christ in their lives and want to share it with others.

They regard their tiny daughter Zoe as the most precious person in their lives. They realize how much love God had for **His** Son, Jesus Christ. They are overwhelmed that He would give His dearly loved Son to die on the cross for them.

There are many skeptics who look at the new Zenon Andrusyshyn and remember the old days. They scoff and snidely comment that "a leopard can't change his spots."

Zee heartily agrees. But then with a wide, thankful smile he says, "But God can!"

Jesus looked at them and said, "With man this is impossible, but with God all things are possible." Matthew 19:26

3

A Rookie Once More
Bernie "Boom Boom" Geoffrion

It was January 1978 and Marlene Geoffrion, with husband Boom Boom away on a business trip, sat down with a cup of coffee to read the Atlanta morning paper. Scanning the sports page, she noticed that Gene Carr of the NHL Atlanta Flames was being sent to the minors, to Atlanta's farm team—Tulsa, Oklahoma, of the Central League.

She suddenly felt sad and truly concerned for Gene's wife, Kathy. A California girl, beautiful and vivacious, she had been literally falling apart from September to December, living with the pressures of being a hockey wife. She was uptight, bitter, very upset and disappointed with the direction of her husband's career.

Marlene had not seen Kathy for some time, but she knew very well the pressures with which she was living. Marlene is as much an NHL veteran as Boom. She is the daughter of the late Howie Morenz, a Montreal legend and hockey hero. She is the wife of a dynamic man who ranks with Rocket Richard as one of the league's all-time great goal scorers and one of the most famous to ever wear the bleu-blanc-rouge of Les Canadiens. She is the mother of Danny Geoffrion, a rookie with the Canadiens, and mother-in-law of Hartland Monohan of the St. Louis Blues, who is married to her daughter, Linda.

Marlene had lived for years with the pressures that Kathy Carr was facing: the long hours alone while her husband was travelling, the fear of serious injury, the tension of being cut or traded, reading the newspapers and listening to the vulgarities shouted at the man she loved, patiently waiting while reporters, fans, and autograph seekers all had first rights to her husband. And finally, after the lights over the shining ice have been turned out, the concessionares departed, walking out into the dark night and an empty parking lot.

To Kathy, it was all new. She was a rookie.

Marlene was thinking of calling her when the doorbell rang. No sooner had she opened it, than in bounced Kathy Carr, with ear to ear teeth!

"Here I was thinking 'poor Kathy,' " Marlene recalls, "and in she walks with this great big smile on her face—so excited, just a totally different person from what I'd just pictured. She had just stopped in to say good-bye as they were getting ready to leave for Tulsa, so we talked about moving and things for about half an hour."

Marlene's curiosity got the best of her; she just had to know what was going on in Kathy's life. What was responsible for the big change—why was she so excited? It just didn't make sense. Kathy's husband was being sent to the minors and **she** was cheering up Marlene?

"What made you change so much?" asked the puzzled Marlene.

"Oh, does it show?" Kathy smiled. "I don't know how to tell you this, Marlene, but I've asked Jesus Christ to come into my life and He has changed me."

Stunned, Marlene could only reply, "Well, that's just terrific."

"By the way," continued Kathy, "I'm going to my last Bible study in Atlanta in the morning. Would you like to come along?"

Marlene thought quickly, "Well, I'm really busy. It's the middle of the week. Boom is out of town, you know, but give me a call in the morning."

Kathy left and Marlene tried to forget about going to the Bible study. "There was just no way I was going to go," remembers Marlene. "Yet, I had to go; I just could not believe how Kathy had changed. I had to find out about this Bible study.

"I was wide awake at 5 a.m. the next morning. I couldn't sleep. As badly as I wanted to go, I just couldn't agree to it. Well, after 14 cups of coffee, Kathy called, and I was ready to go anywhere.

"We drove to Doc Eshelman's and I'll never forget how friendly everyone was—how warm and comfortable the atmosphere was. The leader, Penny Nosette, started to go through the Old Testament, and she asked us to turn to the books she was reading from. I had never heard of them before—how was I supposed to find them? Diane Pronovost, Jean's wife, also of the Flames, was sitting beside me. Sensing my discomfort, she would whisper the page numbers to me in French so I could follow.

"Driving home in the car with Kathy, I realized the Bible had been so fascinating. 'Why hadn't I ever read the Bible?' I wondered. I had always thought I was a Christian, yet I didn't have what these people had," relates Marlene.

Turning to Kathy as they pulled in the driveway, Marlene said, "It doesn't matter how old you are, you are never too old to learn. Kathy, I want Jesus Christ to be my Savior, too."

Kathy exclaimed, "Marlene, I'm so excited; I planted the seed!"

Marlene replied, "I don't know what seed you are talking about, but tell me how to ask Jesus Christ into my life."

Marlene spent the rest of the day thinking. She went out to a bookstore and bought her own Bible and began to read. It would be three days before Boom was due home, and she couldn't wait to tell him what she had done.

Boom Boom Geoffrion is one of the most talented, colorful and dynamic players to ever play in the NHL—league scoring champion (the second man ever to score 50 goals in one season), perennial All-Star and hockey's diplomat. He retired from the Canadiens in 1964, after 16 seasons, and went to the Quebec Aces of the American Hockey League to learn the coaching skills he hoped would enable him to return to the NHL.

Two years later, after finishing first both seasons but failing to win the Calder Cup awarded to the league champions, he was dismissed. Tired of trying to ask his players to play his way, he decided to show them his way. He returned as a player to the New York Rangers, even though during training camp "I thought I was going to die," he states. He showed them how to win, spreading the pride he had acquired from his years with Les Canadiens.

Plagued with a bleeding ulcer, he resigned as a

player after two seasons to coach the Rangers for Emile Francis. After only half a season, his health caused him to call it quits.

The Atlanta Flames chose him to coach the expansion team in 1972. Boomer reacted to Atlanta in the same way Atlanta did to Boomer—it was love at first sight. In later years he became vice president of promotion. His job: sell hockey to the football-, baseball-, and basketball-crazy city of Atlanta. He worked as hard trying to sell the game and put people in the seats at the Omni as he had in his playing days for the Canadiens. His long-dreamed-of coaching job with the Canadiens and the Flames move to Calgary were far in the future as he returned from his business trip to his excited wife.

"Marlene told me that she had been to a Bible study and she had asked Jesus Christ into her life," states Boom. "I didn't really understand or say anything, but over the next couple of weeks I noticed a real change in her. She was always smiling and happy. When she asked me to go with her one night to Ed Kea's, I agreed. I already knew a lot of things they were talking about but I found the Bible pretty interesting. Ed suggested I attend a conference in Phoenix, Arizona, sponsored by Professional Athletes Outreach, but I wasn't too interested."

Boom had told Marlene that she could choose where they would go on holidays. She began to leave books and pamphlets all over the house. "Anywhere he sat down: the kitchen, the living room, the bedroom, the den, the bathroom, I made sure there was something there for him to read about the conference," smiles Marlene.

Boom left on another speaking trip. "Each time he would call home, Boom would tell me how interesting some book about Christian athletes was—and this from a man who used to read one book a year, if that," states Marlene.

One athlete in particular had made a lasting impression—Ron Pritchard of the Cincinnati Bengals of the National Football League. When Boom and Marlene showed up at the Phoenix conference, who was the guest speaker? Ron Pritchard.

"I guess I was surprised!" remembers Geoffrion. "I knew him as a great football player, and really enjoyed his talk. He tells it like it is. I went up to congratulate him after the banquet and he surprised me."

Ron looked squarely at the Boomer and said, "What about you, Boom, have you asked Jesus Christ into your life?"

Boom quickly repli⌐ "Well, that's great for you, but I'm not ready for that now, maybe tomorrow."

How many men put off until tomorrow what should be done today? How many take for granted there will be a tomorrow in their life? Yesterday is gone, tomorrow may never be, but we have today! Boom agreed to go for a walk with Ron in the Phoenix night.

"I prayed with Ron on the sidewalk to ask Jesus Christ to save me," states Boom. "I couldn't believe it was so simple. I asked him if that was all there was to it."

"Yes," Ron replied. "God will now start to work in your life."

Work He did. Boom was never much of a church-goer, but now he was like an eager rookie all over again. "Now I can't wait to get there on Sunday. Sometimes I spend five hours there."

Sounds like the Boomer of old who would be in the dressing room at the Forum at five o'clock for an eight o'clock game.

The Geoffrions were very happy in Atlanta. Boom Boom was a household word, they had a beautiful home and the climate was ideal. Nothing could make them move—that is, nothing except the opportunity to coach the Montreal Canadiens.

When Boom was approached about the vacancy created by Scotty Bowman going to the Buffalo Sabres, the old fires and dreams began to grow. The money would be great; the Canadiens coaching job would fulfill a desire long ago stifled in Quebec City. This was not just any coaching job, it was the Canadiens. There are many who think that Geoffrion has no heart—it's just a big Canadien's crest inside his rib cage. So Boomer and Marlene headed back to Montreal. It was, in Boomer's words at the time, "A dream come true."

The pressure was intense from day one. Several key players had left the defending Stanley Cup champs. An intense rivalry had been created with the Quebec Nordiques coming into the league. Boom thrived on it as any good athlete does—pressure makes the cream come to the top in athletics. There was one major problem: his success was not dependent upon **his** performance—it was dependent on his players' performance.

Boom Boom was confused. Attitudes had changed. It was no longer the Canadien dressing room he had so loved. Modern athletes with large contracts play to live—Boomer had lived to play! Pride had always been a tradition with the Canadiens. In his day they were dedicated to winning. Once, soon after suffering a ruptured spleen in practice and almost dying, Boom sneaked back to the Forum to practice so Marlene would not find out. When she saw him on the ice, it was too late, and he went on to score two power-play goals to eliminate the Detroit Red Wings in the Stanley Cup play-offs. Another time, Boom and Doug Harvey sat up all night in the washroom of a train, wittling a cast off an injured knee so he could play the next day against the Chicago Black Hawks in a Stanley Cup semi-final series. They had **practiced** more intently and more seriously than other teams **played**.

The schedule wore on. Team meetings produced no results. Boom lost weight. He became frustrated. The team played poorly at home. Slowly, Boom began to realize that his cherished dream was not all that rosy.

He didn't say anything to Marlene about resigning, since he felt she would be disappointed. Marlene did not express her feelings to Boom about resigning, since she felt he would be disappointed. As well, Boom was growing distant from two very important people in his life.

"I wanted to be closer to Jesus Christ," he recalls. "My son Danny and I had our problems, too. It just killed me to tell him he wouldn't be dressing. Here I was a proud father with a son who was a rookie with the Canadiens, and I had to tell him he couldn't play.

"I was starting to swear again and do a lot of things I used to; I did not like the person I was becoming. I missed my fellowship with other Christians.

"I finally told Marlene, 'Enough is enough.' I went into the front office to hand in my resignation, and we were on our way home to Atlanta the same day."

Marlene adds, "We were just like a couple of

excited kids packing our suitcases." The man who had given hockey the slapshot and thousands of thrills, a member of the Hockey Hall of Fame, had finally found peace.

One cannot come into contact with Boom Boom Geoffrion and not be affected. He gets so excited talking about the glory days of Les Canadiens. To really see him glow and shine and get excited though, ask him to read the Bible to you! Boom Boom is no theologian; he is an excited and hungry rookie Christian. But that doesn't stop him from telling anyone who will listen about what his Lord Jesus Christ has done for him.

I will instruct you and teach you in the way you should go; I will counsel you and watch over you.   **Psalm 32:8**

4

The Road to Salvation
Jennifer Diachun Palmer

Jennifer Diachun waited impatiently to enter the stadium for the 1968 Olympic Games. Long lines held the hundreds of athletes representing countries from all over the world. Since arriving in Mexico City, she had grown increasingly frustrated as organizers battled the language difficulties and obstacles that the sheer numbers of people presented. But Jennifer's physical training and mental preparation were at a peak. Beginning the following day, she would represent her country against the finest women gymnasts in the world.

Finally, the time arrived for the athletes to begin their ceremonial walk around the stadium. Fourteen-year-old Jennifer was very tired as she fell in step with her teammates and began to walk down the path towards the entrance way.

"As we walked, I could hear the cheers and the music and excitement generated by the countries that entered ahead of us," remembers Jenny. "What followed was incredible. I looked up and the stadium was packed. Canadian music was playing, and Canadian flags were waving to us from this huge mass of people. I was overwhelmed by the support we were being given. I got so excited and began to cry with joy.''

This was the culmination of years of preparation and unexpected success.

The preparation was not all physical—there had been legal problems to overcome as well. Jennifer was required to sign a form stating that the Olympic committee would not be responsible for her in any way—she was a year below the minimum age to compete in the Olympic Games.

But that was common in women's gymnastics—a sport in which all the women are small and young. As the female body matures and develops, it becomes more difficult to control due to a marked change in the strength-to-weight ratio. Thus, the peak years for a female gymnast are her teen years. It is an amazing paradox, for while a teenage gymnast is at her peak physically, emotionally she is at a very tender age when she must handle the pressures of competing at the Olympic level of performance.

Jenny, although not a medal winner, was the highest scoring Canadian competitor on the women's gymnastics team.

Most athletes are drawn to higher levels of competition by initially attracting attention with superior performance in their sport. But Jenny's debut was anything but a spectacular performance.

"I was nine years old and I did handstands in the living room of our home in Toronto," Jenny recalls. "Then I lost my balance and knocked over my mother's prized table. Shattered glass flew all over the room, and I cried and cried. My mother felt I had so much energy that I should have something to direct it at—other than her furniture. When a friend suggested gymnastics, gymnastics it was. I joined some exercise classes and was promptly given the nickname 'Spider' because I was just a skinny little kid with the boniest knees you could ever imagine.''

Jenny's promising talents soon emerged and private instruction and competition challenged her and aided her development. Attending Camp Olympia in Baton Rouge, Louisiana, she came under the excellent teaching of the 1964 U.S. Olympic coach Vannie Edwards. In 1967, she became a member of the Scarborough Winstonette Gymnastic Club, then the highest ranked club for female gymnasts in Canada. She placed second in the Quebec Winter Games, and won four gold medals in the junior calibre level of the Canadian Championships, held at the Canadian National Exhibition in Toronto, August 1967.

Nineteen sixty-eight was Olympic year, and the trials to determine who would represent Canada in Mexico took place from May through July. Although she was a junior competitor, it was decided Jenny could benefit from the exposure and experience of the trials.

''I entered the senior events for fun, to see how well I would do,'' says Jenny.

Looking at the results, she did rather well, to say the least. Jenny finished second overall on the basis of her performance in three trials. She was assured an automatic berth on Canada's Olympic team. From a sloppy handstand in her living room, Jenny moved to the center stage of international competition in just five years.

Gymnasts compete in a sport requiring incredible precision. Their concentration has to be unshakeable, their training intense. Gymnasts routinely perform movements that are extremely dangerous. They make everything seem so simple to the casual observer.

"There were countless numbers of hours spent in training that cut into areas of my life that other people would cherish. For example, my social life. I went through a lot of tears and pain and fatigue, just as any other athlete does. Yet it was all truly worth it. I've met people all over the world who are my friends for life. I have learned discipline, sportsmanship, how to deal with winning and losing and how to endure hardships. I was never forced to compete, and continued only because I liked it so much. I would watch people's faces as I did my floor exercises, and it was so much fun for me to see the enjoyment and excitement they were getting from me. As far as I'm concerned, I have not missed a thing in my life; I have only profited."

Jenny's career continued. In June of 1969, she returned to Mexico City to compete against Cuba, Mexico, and the U.S. in the Cup of America Championships, winning a gold medal in the vault. The World Games in Yugoslavia in 1970 and the Pan Am Games in Cali, Columbia, increased her competitive edge. Nineteen seventy-two was Olympic year in Munich, a special year as all six female gymnasts were from the same club. In 1973 Jenny captured a gold medal on the balance beam at the South American Invitational. Moscow and Bulgaria in 1973 and 1974 for the University and World Games, respectively, rounded out her world travel.

"I was thinking about retiring in 1973," recalls Jenny. "I wanted to retire a champion and win the Canadian Nationals. I trained so hard and so long."

Athletes in a team sport can have a weak moment, shift, period, or perhaps a whole game. There is always a teammate to cover up for them—someone else to carry the workload if they fail. Gymnasts do not have that luxury. They compete in a sport in which one slip can mean automatic defeat, a sport in which margins of defeat are measured in hundredths of a point. They must try to concentrate while music blares for another gymnast doing floor exercises—someone else hits the springboard for a vault—the crowd reacts to a score given to another competitor. While all this is going on, the gymnast stands alone, with no teammate to help.

Jenny, hoping to retire a winner, lost the Nationals by one one-hundredth of a point. "It was the biggest disappointment of my career; my pride was really hurt," recalls Jenny.

Many people accept mediocrity and failure in their lives with "if." It is the most revealing word to come from the mouth of a loser, whether in life or in sport. The truth, though, is that it is the "doers," and not the "iffers," who bathe in the spotlight of victory and success. The brightest stars shine in the darkest night, and it was in her darkest defeat that Jenny shone. She realized that she was being given an opportunity to grow through her adversity.

"Under Coach Brian McVey, I trained and worked harder than I ever had before. I was going to take another shot at the Nationals the following year. I spent 4 to 5 hours a night after school practicing. There were times when I was thoroughly exhausted. I would be caked with chalk dust. I'd have blisters. My muscles would be sore and my hips would be bruised from the uneven bars. I kept going, though, and I soon began to develop a real sense of self-satisfaction. I was in top shape, super fit. I gained a lot of confidence and really began to enjoy my training."

Her hard work paid off. Jenny became the next National Champion.

Her final competition was in Maple Leaf Gardens in 1974. There she tied with the Soviet Union's World Champion, Nelli Kim. Colin Wackett of the Ontario Gymnastics Federation was a featured speaker at a dinner honoring the accomplishments of the retiring young athlete. He recalled Jenny's tenth birthday, a big day in a Ukrainian household—he was one of the 30 cousins commandeered by Jenny's mother. Uncles, aunts...everyone had to sit and watch Jenny's routine on the balance beam in the backyard. Colin remembered how proud her parents were, but also how terrible Jenny was. All the relatives were embarrassed. At that time, Colin could not believe Jenny's proud mom saying, "She's going to be in the Olympics."

Now he was one of many honoring her for, among many other accomplishments, being an Olympian.

It was New Year's Eve, 1974. A good friend of Jenny's, Zenon Andrusyshyn, arranged a blind date for Jenny with Peter Palmer of the B.C. Lions of the Canadian Football League. Now six years later, residing in Richmond, B.C., she and Peter await the arrival of their first child. And Jenny has her own gymnastics club, coaching about 30 children.

"Gymnastics is such a big part of my life, I don't know what I would do without it," says Jenny. "I love coaching and I want to be the best coach I am capable of being."

The Thompson Gymnastic Club is not her only

concern. She is also a physiotherapist involved with rehabilitation medicine in the Clyde Smith Sports Medicine Clinic in Vancouver. To make sure they don't waste any time, Peter and Jenny also operate their own marketing and management business in Richmond, Turn Point International.

A successful sports career, marriage and family, coaching and business involvements—these are only half of Jenny's story. There is a spiritual story to be told as well, one that started years earlier.

Before every competition, Jenny prayed a little prayer ending with the words, "Show me the road to salvation." It took a long time, and a lot of tears. When she was shown the way, she refused to accept it. But God does answer prayers, and His delays are not His denials.

"Peter had become a Christian and we attended an Athletes In Action conference in 1975. It was just terrible," recalls Jenny. "I had never experienced anything like it. It was totally foreign to me, the concept of having a personal relationship with the Lord Jesus Christ. I had been raised in a religious background, but I had never heard anything like this before. I was really upset and intimidated, and couldn't wait to get out of there."

Jenny made an excuse not to attend the 1976 conference, but by 1977 she had gotten to know many other Christian athletes. She realized what a difference it made to other couples to have Jesus Christ as the head of their marriages.

"I also noticed that while Peter was always calm, cool and collected, I was the world's worst worry wart. I had always worried about everything—my career, my family, my studies. You name it, and I worried about it. I often wondered about Peter's inner strength."

So when the 1977 conference came up, Jenny agreed to go with Peter.

"I listened to the speaker and I just couldn't go to sleep that night. I was upset and crying. Finally, about four o'clock in the morning, I woke Peter up and started asking him questions. I wanted to know who this Lord was and why He had come. Why had I never known about all this before? I wanted to know what I was missing out on. Peter and I talked for quite awhile, and then we prayed together. I wanted to meet the Lord Jesus Christ as my Savior.

"A lot of people don't feel any different—but I sure felt different. I had bells ringing. I was so excited and I was crying. I couldn't sleep the rest of the night. The next morning, I told everyone I ran into that I was one of God's children, and He had chosen me. I was so happy!"

Prior to the morning session, time was set aside for anyone who wanted to share what Jesus Christ was doing in his life. Until then, Jenny had always had to listen to others. But now she bounded up to the microphone to tell what Jesus Christ had done in **her** life.

"I got about five words out and I started crying again. I was crying, everybody else was crying, and Peter had to finish for me. It was the greatest experience ever in my whole life, and I just could not contain the joy I felt."

Tears come easily for Jenny Palmer. But now that she has found the "road to salvation" she searched for for so many years, they are tears of joy.

And without faith it is impossible to please God, because anyone who comes to him must believe that he exists and that he rewards those who earnestly seek him. Hebrews 11:6

5

Lineman From the Bayou
Ron "Swamp Dawg" Estay

The hospital had a distinguished patient. The folks in Baton Rouge, Louisiana, loved their Louisiana State University football players. One of their best was recovering from wrist surgery while in the thick of a long and star-studded career. Known as "Crockett," he stretched out his 6'1" 240 lb. frame, relaxed and reflected back on his college career.

Just graduated with a bachelor of science degree in physical education and social studies, drafted by the Denver Broncos of the National Football League, ABC-TV's defensive player of the year, **Sports Illustrated**'s lineman of the week, two-time All-American, Vince Lombardi top college lineman in the country runner-up—he was a young man who had caught the attention of the sporting world and was on his way up. Ron Estay smiled and felt pretty special.

Seems someone else thought he was special also. Coach Eagle Keyes had travelled all the way from Vancouver, British Columbia, to visit and persuade this valuable piece of football property to play for the British Columbia Lions of the Canadian Football

League. The offer proved too attractive to refuse. A one year no-cut contract with a guaranteed starting position and some fine salesmanship convinced the Louisiana Bayou product to return to the country of his Cajun roots. The pride of Baton Rouge slipped through the fingers of the NFL and migrated north of the 49th parallel.

Once in Vancouver, he explored his new lifestyle and sought acceptance from his teammates. He was truly one of the boys and lived life to the hilt.

"I had a wild and wooly image to live up to and did anything that would support it," recalls Ron.

Since his college days, Ron had lived hard to try to forget earlier tragedy in his life. Now he was a pro rookie with money to burn and time to kill. He was just as active off the field as he was on—anything for kicks, with an eye out for a new thrill, whether it be fighting, drinking or carousing. "I was the toast of the town and on top of the mountain."

Early in his second season, no longer protected by the no-cut clause, Ron was named defensive player of the game. But immediately after, the usual locker room excitement was shattered. Coach Keyes told him he was no longer needed, no longer a part of the team. His off-the-field actions had cost him his on-the-field job.

"I was shocked. For years I had seen hundreds of other guys clean out their lockers—but I never thought it would happen to me."

Hurt and embarrassed, his ego and identity tied to football, he swallowed his pride and crossed the Rockies to the Alberta home of the Edmonton Eskimos. His new teammates affectionately nicknamed him "Swamp Dawg" because of his background and love for hunting. He worked hard to re-establish himself and regain his confidence. By the end of the season he was defensive captain and the Eskimos were in the 1973 Grey Cup.

Meanwhile, a new teammate had become very influential in his life. Whenever he had the chance, Gary Lefebvre would talk to Ron about Jesus Christ.

"My wife Debbie had become a born again Christian, and she kept telling Gary to talk to me. Gary never let up," Ron recalls. "Every day he'd be after me, until I couldn't take it anymore and I angrily told him to quit bugging me.

"But I sensed Gary and my other Christian teammates really did have something different in their lives. Inside I wanted to ask questions, wanted what they had—but I was afraid to ask and show that I was interested. Inside I was troubled; I had always thought I was a Christian, had always been told I was a Christian. I had been raised in a religious home. Yet I knew very little about Jesus Christ. My doubt, past personal tragedy, and my pride caused me to ignore what Gary had to say."

Life as Ron knew it didn't seem to have any place for religion. He belonged to the tough and violent world of pro football. A game in which size, strength, intimidation, inflated egos, and mental and physical toughness were basic tools of the trade. Humility was a sign of weakness, so he couldn't see his career being helped by adopting a humble, Christian way of life. He had once come very close to losing his career. But he had had an excellent season, had his confidence back, and was not going to do anything to risk losing it again. Because of the Vancouver episode, Ron had eaten a lot of crow and did not like the taste of it.

"As much as I wanted this strange new life, there was too much pride in the way," he recalls.

But he could not deny the fact that he did admire these guys who talked about Jesus Christ, if only inwardly and secretly. "I remember Mike Wilson of the Lions as being a true friend. Mike would come over and baby-sit while Debbie would go to a Bible study and I would go drinking."

Ron did reluctantly agree to go to a Bible study with Gary, Mike Lambros and Sam Britts. He was excited about what he heard and impressed because the guys were able to understand the Bible. With some friendly prodding and Debbie's arranging, Ron agreed to attend an Athletes In Action Pro Conference in Chicago, 1974. He had never been to the big city and was not prepared to meet the three big men he did: NFL veterans Mike McCoy and Norm Evans and his Savior Jesus Christ.

"I had always equated Christianity with weakness. I just stared as McCoy, 6'7" 300 lbs., and Evans, 6'5" 290 lbs., told of how they needed Jesus Christ in their lives, and how their lives had been changed. Suddenly I understood; I realized how great a man Jesus was, to have suffered what He did on the cross."

He humbly bowed his head to Somebody greater than he ever could expect to be. He asked Jesus Christ to save him, for he realized that the debt of his sin was so great that he could never pay it himself. Ron's new life had begun. He was reborn. He was alive spiritually.

The life of spiritual deadness that had just ended began in rural Louisiana—a sportsman's paradise where Ron grew up hunting and fishing with his grandfather, father and two older brothers.

"It put food on the table and provided a closeness amongst the men in the family," Ron remembers.

Life was simple. His older brother was already a star at LSU, and Ron and his Dad cherished the times going up to Baton Rouge to watch him play. "Someday," Ron vowed, "I was going to follow in their footsteps."

Then the first of a series of family tragedies took place. When Ron was twelve his grandfather died very suddenly and unexpectedly of tuberculosis. Three years later, one of his two older football-playing brothers was killed in an auto accident. Within a short time, his grandmother died.

But the incident that really hurt was his father collapsing during Labor Day weekend and being taken to the hospital for examination, revealing terminal bone cancer.

"For three months I watched my father waste away. I buried my dad in November."

Heartbroken, bitter, angry, cheated, confused—no words can describe the hurt of a teenager who loses a dearly loved parent.

"Why would God do this; why is He so cruel? Why? Why? Why?" Ron asked for answers and never got them. He would often sit in the dressing room after a game and cry in self-pity.

"I wanted so much for my dad to be able to share in my success. I knew how much he had enjoyed the game, the excitement, the joy of watching his sons out on the field." But Ron never had the privilege, that warm feeling of looking up in the stands and knowing his dad was watching. He began to live hard to try to forget.

If only someone had told him then what he knows now as a Christian. God is not to blame for death.

Death is a result of sin and is from the devil—not God.

"I know now that Jesus Christ conquered death when He rose from the grave. He took the sting out of death for all those who have believed on Him."

It is similar to running down the field, catching a pass off balance, turning and suddenly realizing from the look in the tackler's eyes, his speed, and his size, that you are going to get hit like you've never been hit before. It's inevitable, there's no escape, you're going to get it! In that split second you decide to make him pay a price to hit you. Every ounce of physical strength inside all that padding explodes as you fight back at impact. Just as quickly it's over. You've been hit like you've never been hit—**But** you're OK! You've taken the guy's best shot and you're OK! As you get up, you smile, grab his hand and say, "Good hit—but not good enough!!" You run off, the adrenalin pumping, your heart pounding. Look over your shoulder and you see a look of anger and frustration on the face of the guy who thought he was going to destroy you. That is what death will be like for anyone protected by Christ. He has taken the devil's best shot for you, and laughed in his face.

Ron's life has changed considerably. "Without Jesus Christ," Ron openly admits, "I'd be divorced, probably in jail and certainly wouldn't be playing football."

With his wife, Debbie, and children, Brannon and Angela, Ron makes his year-round home in Edmonton. "I hunt quarterbacks for a living and big game for a hobby." There is still the occasional trip back to the Bayou to hunt ducks and visit his mom—who has also come to know Jesus Christ.

"Swamp" is back on top of the mountain. This time it is a real mountain, unshakeable. Life is sweet. There's lots of love to be shared with family and teammates. Success is ever present playing for the Eskimos, appearing in six out of seven Grey Cups and winning three. But most of all, a new power source is there from which to draw: Jesus Christ.

Named Players' Association defensive lineman of the year and CFL All-Pro and Western Conference All-Star, he is reaping the benefits of an industrious career and a successful team.

Don't be surprised if some night you are watching a post-game interview and hear a quarterback describe what it feels like to be steamrolled by a charging "Swamp Dawg." The bewildered player doesn't know what makes a bigger impact on him, being pounded physically or spiritually, as No. 55 reaches down and helps him shake the cobwebs out of his head. "Just doing my job. And remember, Jesus loves you and so do I."

If you think you're tough, I suggest you speak with Ron Estay. If you think Ron Estay is tough, he'll suggest you "speak with Jesus Christ!"

...but those who hope in the Lord will renew their strength. They will soar on wings like eagles; they will run and not grow weary.
Isaiah 40:31

6

Waiting for the Comeback
Pat Bonnett

The 1979 Grey Cup was a frustrating and emotional day for Montreal Alouette fans and players alike. The Als just could not get anything going all afternoon and the Edmonton Eskimos repeatedly throttled the Montreal offensive thrust. The minutes ticked off the scoreboard clock, yet everyone in the stadium hoped for a last-minute Alouette comeback.

Suddenly, a glimmer of hope appeared. The fans jumped to their feet, cheering wildly as Keith Baker of the Alouettes caught a punt and headed for the Eskimo goal line. The yards were gobbled up by the fleet runner following his blockers, and the referee signalled touchdown Montreal. New life, new hope; nervous eyes glanced at the clock. There was still time for…a red penalty flag had been thrown against Montreal, the sweet taste of victory turned sour and the touchdown was called back.

Instantly, the television cameras flashed to the Alouette bench. Millions of people across the country came face to face with a lonely and hurting figure on the sidelines. His eyes brimming with tears, 6'2'' - 240 lb. offensive guard Pat Bonnett stood in his streetclothes, shifting his weight uneasily as he felt stabs of pain from the left knee that kept him out of the game. All the emotional and physical pain that had built up for months sought release in the tears he fought to hold back, biting his lip.

"I just felt so helpless; I felt so sorry for my teammates. They tried and tried and tried all day, yet they couldn't get things to come together. It was so frustrating and discouraging," remembers Bonnett. "Most fans get the feeling a player just goes out to hit or run or catch. It's just not that mechanical. There is a lot more mental and emotional preparation than meets the eye. Some players try to live up to an image created by others, but most players are sensitive family men—normal human beings, and it was a very frustrating experience."

Adding to the frustration were memories of the previous year's Grey Cup in the Olympic stadium—also a Montreal versus Edmonton match-up. It was the culmination of Pat's finest moments as a pro football player. "It was the first game in the Olympic stadium, and everyone was caught up in the excitement. We had had a very successful season as a team and we were going to play against our arch rivals, the Eskimos, in front of our own home fans. The fans, media, coaches, players and the whole city were really excited. During the season Edmonton had trounced us good."

But now Montreal had Grey Cup fever.

The weather had not cooperated. The Grey Cup finale has been played in almost any weather condition possible: rain, snow, fog—and that year it was to be ice. The entire field could have been used for a practice session for the Montreal Canadiens. Embroiled in controversy because of the poor field conditions, the game was played and the Alouettes came out victorious with a very convincing win.

"The game and the whole year leading up to it was the most significant athletic highlight of my life," recalls Pat. "We had an advantage because very early in the game, I and the other offensive linemen noticed that when we ran our plays in one direction we had good traction, while if we went the other way, we had to be a little more cautious and careful. We relayed the information to the coaches and adjusted accordingly.

"The reason for the difference in traction was that the artificial turf was also used as the playing field for the Montreal Expos of the National Baseball League. The turf was laid in such a manner as to provide non-friction for ground balls. Realizing that we could go in one direction easier than the other, we adjusted our take-off from the line."

Between the two tension-packed Grey Cups, Pat was to experience the possible end of his seven-year pro career. In a game against the Ottawa Rough Riders in August of 1979, he was seriously injured with only three minutes left to play in the game. Blocked on the play, he felt his left knee give in.

Knees are as important to an athlete as string to a yo-yo. Three long bones meet to form the knee joint, one of which, the femur or thigh bone, is the largest in the human body. Discs of cartilage and a lubricating fluid prevent the ends of each bone from grinding and rubbing together. Holding the joint together are tiny ligaments stretching from bone to bone. Muscle tendons bind as they pass over the joint. Most fragile, this nevertheless is the area that is subject to heavy pounding and twisting in a contact sport. Torn ligaments or cartilage allow the bones to move from their natural resting place, causing the rupture of the capsule. Blood and fluid escape and the knee swells.

Pat's knee received a blow or pressure from the outside which his leg muscles could not contain. Because of the force of the blow, the ligament on the inside of his knee tore away from the bone, allowing the bones to shift.

"There wasn't a lot of immediate pain," remembers Pat, "but I just knew there was something wrong. I didn't bother going downfield, I limped to the bench."

Pat underwent surgery the same evening. The ligament was stapled to the bone. Told the next day he could expect to be back by the end of the season, he soon began the endless weeks of therapy.

"I regularly went to the trainer's room and for 5-6 hours a day would try to regain flexibility using a whirlpool, forcing the leg to bend. The thigh muscles had begun to shrink with non-use and I lifted light weights to retain my leg strength. It was very, very painful, but I knew if I wanted to come back, I would have to go through it."

Forced inactivity because of injury is trying for an athlete. The emotional damage can be as damaging as the physical. He is suddenly an outsider. While he is in the locker room, his teammates are on the field. He no longer contributes, and even though intellectually he knows he is a part of the team, he feels he is not. Teammates unconsciously react as well, for they recognize in the injured player something that could very easily happen to them. To avoid confronting this possibility, many players may soon begin to reject the injured teammate.

"I soon realized that I wasn't going to make it by the end of the season, so we aimed at being ready for the Grey Cup," remembers Pat.

But his optimism proved faulty, and a lonely figure on the sidelines watched his team go down to defeat.

With the frustrating loss behind him, Pat began to prepare for the opening of training camp in June. He jogged over Christmas but the pain would not disappear. X-rays and examination revealed that the staples that had been inserted to hold the ligament to the bone had moved. They would eventually have to be removed.

On January 31, 1980, a second operation was performed. The therapy began all over again. Everything gained had been lost.

"My knee continued to swell and stiffen. They put a scope inside the joint and discovered there was cartilage damage and that arthritis had begun to develop."

On March 28, the knee underwent a third operation to correct the condition. "By this time, not only training camp was out the window, but also the CFL season. Coach Scannella was very supportive during the ordeal, but we both agreed it would be best to sit out the season."

It was a jarring halt to a career that included five Grey Cup games, winning two. Yet there is so much more to that career. One must look past the statistics and record books to seek the man who, in spite of all his suffering, is not destroyed.

What type of man can accept his misfortune as being an ordered part of his life, who can calmly say, "If the knee progresses as it should, I'll try again"? Who or what can claim the credit for Pat Bonnett's inner strength and peace?

In June of 1973, a homegrown product of Montreal who had recently graduated from Idaho State University of the Big Sky Football Conference, attended his first pro camp. The media and head coach Marv Levy were duly impressed by the big rookie with the big attitude. It wasn't long before he was interviewed; the headline in the Montreal daily paper read "BONNETT CREDITS CHRIST." Pat Bonnett was back in town.

He had left in 1968 to attend Idaho State on an athletic scholarship. "I felt very successful," recalls Pat. "I had everything going for me. I enjoyed athletics and was well accepted by my friends. Academics was never a real problem. Yet when I went home at Christmas of my first year, I told my parents I wanted to quit. I found university life did not satisfy me and did not meet my expectations. I had already accomplished a number of things and at that point I hadn't thought much about playing pro football. I had never followed it that much and it wasn't a great passion in my life. I had been playing since I was 13 years old and had become involved only because some friends urged me because of my size. Being away from home, I also realized how significant money was in people's lives. People did crazy things to get it, and their whole lives were preoccupied with spending it. I really questioned where it all would lead to and if that was to be my purpose in life. My parents encouraged me to stay in university, but left the decision up to me. I realized that it was a critical point in my life, but I had never given up, I had never quit in anything I'd ever done. So I returned to Idaho State to complete the year. If I was still dissatisfied, I knew I could at least transfer my credits.''

Pat was undergoing a lot of personal growth and questioning. Thrust into a major campus at sixteen years of age, he was exposed to a new environment and found himself in conflict with the moral standards expected of him. How much would he have to change to be accepted? As well, as an outstanding high school athlete, he was a big fish in a little pond; here the roles were reversed—he was just one of 7,000 students. He would often climb into the surrounding mountains and choose a spot where he could see no one in any direction. It was a strange feeling.

''I felt terribly alone in the mountains. And yet I could be in a study hall, a lecture room, or at a party and still feel the same way, surrounded by people.''

Then Pat met a friend who belonged to Campus Crusade for Christ. ''We talked,'' recalls Pat, ''but I avoided the guy like the plague. One Friday night he asked me if I was doing anything and I remember thinking I really blew it when I said no. Well, he invited me to a gathering and I figured it wouldn't last that long, so I decided to attend. I was really interested in what made them tick. Why would a group of teenagers want to sing songs and talk about God on a Friday night? I had always considered religion as something you did on Sundays, and that you only prayed at night with the lights out. I was impressed with what I saw; everyone seemed to have a joy, a peace, a sense of purpose. We discussed a number of things, and then he asked me if I wanted to accept Jesus Christ as my Savior. I swallowed my pride and prayed in front of 15 or 20 people. I prayed that Jesus would become real and personal to me. I immediately knew I would never be alone again.''

Pat began attending Bible studies, and it was there he met his future wife, Renee. About that time, the football team had come under close scrutiny regarding hair. The coaches decreed no long hair, no beards, no moustaches, no goatees. "We figured, why not shave it all off? We had a hair-cutting party, and 75 football players were walking around campus bald-headed. It was great for team unity," laughs Pat.

Renee had always been a little intimidated by athletes anyway, and this incident did nothing to alter her already poor impression. She was quite stunned to find two of those bald heads in her Bible study group in the fall of 1970. But she married the bald-headed guy in the back of the class, Pat Bonnett, in 1974.

Since joining the Alouettes in Montreal, Pat has been widely involved in various activities. He was on the Board of Directors with Don Liesemer of Hockey Ministries International, setting up chapels in the NHL and running summer camps for boys between the ages of ten and sixteen. He was also chaplain in Archambault Maximum Security Federal Penitentiary. "One of the greatest joys I had was meeting a new Christian, who had been in prison for years. In the midst of all the depressing aspects of prison life, this man shared how his first Christmas as a Christian, even though in prison, had meant so much more to him than any other."

Just as Pat's Christian activities and faith have not isolated him from difficulties in his football career, his home life has not been without trials.

The Bonnett's have two children: Aaron, the younger, and Trish, who was born and almost died on February 17, 1977. After a complicated pregnancy and emergency Caesarean delivery, Trish emerged into the world with her lower spine not fully formed and lying outside her body. Her heartbeat dropped to near fatal level and her skull was abnormally small.

Neurosurgeons advised the young parents she would certainly die if the deformed spinal column and cord were not put in their natural resting place in the body. But returning the spinal column to its natural resting place would not solve the problem—it would remain deformed. About 90 percent of children born with this defect eventually suffer enlarged heads due to fluid on the brain. Because of the location of the damage, she could possibly suffer leg paralysis and, eventually, would most certainly have no control over bladder and kidney functions. There was no surgery to correct the malformation of the spinal column itself; the best they could do would be to put the spinal column inside the body and stitch her up, decreasing the chances of infection, but increasing the possibility of nerve damage by handling the tiny exposed nerves and spinal cord. It was patchwork only.

"I had to make a decision with a life that was 16 hours old," Pat recalls. "I believed this life was created for a purpose and we would never know unless we operated, despite the danger and risk involved. We gave the doctor permission to operate and we told him of the many people who were aware of the situation who would be praying for him and his staff."

Trish spent two hours on the operating table. She was now almost a day old. Complications set in after surgery and the situation looked very grim. Pat finally left the hospital at 3 a.m., and getting into his car, he stopped to pray.

"I just sensed there was a real struggle going on for Trish's life. I asked God to touch and minister to the delicate and precious little life He had given us to love—the creation we were to teach to love and worship and serve her Creator."

Returning to the hospital in the morning, Pat was relieved to see Trish calmed down. Renee spent day and night by Trish's bedside, nursing the little girl entrusted to them.

Despite all predictions, Trish's brain never did swell up; she never did have any bladder or kidney problems. The doctors call her the miracle baby and have told her parents to quit bringing her back to Montreal Children's Hospital for check-ups—she doesn't need them.

Is she normal? "Are you kidding?! She's not normal, she's great," replies Pat, as Trish walks and runs and plays like any other healthy three-year-old girl.

Now in his year off from active duty with the Montreal Alouettes, Pat is an assistant coach at Simon Fraser University in Burnaby, B.C. While there he will be able to utilize the excellent rehabilitative facilities the university has to offer.

"I don't regret a moment of the time I spent in pro ball," he says, "and I will try to return. If I am unable to, I will be just as excited about the new direction my life will take. I look back on all those exciting moments and thrills and I realize that they will all fade away. I've got everything in perspective; I'm investing all my resources into the Word of God—that will last forever.

"I know I was a better athlete as a Christian. There were many times when I would be hurt or tired or the team would be behind. Practices would be long and maybe it would be hard to accept a coach's tongue-lashing. If I had gone through that as a non-Christian, I would have only myself to please and I would be satisfied—I had given enough. But as a Christian, I want to please God by my behavior and so the price is never too high.''

The Simon Fraser University Clansmen football team is in for a rich and rewarding season. They will never tire of exploring the depth of their new coach—the man they saw on national television unashamedly crying on the sidelines of the 1979 Grey Cup.

Pat Bonnett is a man with a future. In his own words, ''I may never play another down of football, but I know that I can still be all that God wants me to be.''

Have I not commanded you? Be strong and courageous. Do not be terrified; do not be discouraged, for the Lord your God will be with you wherever you go.''   Joshua 1:9

7

The Search for Security
Harry Sheehy

Williams College has the kind of atmosphere that would appeal to F. Scott Fitzgerald. Situated in Berkshire Hills, Massachusetts, Williams is a prestigious New England university with a strong academic reputation and an ideal campus setting. In 1972, Harry Sheehy III was a 6'5", 180-pound guard on the Williams College Varsity basketball team.

Harry's roommates had as much class as the campus: Bob Samuelson, whose father Paul won the Nobel Prize in 1970 for his work in economics; and Samuel Bronfmann, who would be kidnapped in 1975 for a $4.5 million ransom.

Harry chose Williams because of its beautiful campus and also because it was his father's alma mater. He was following in his dad's footsteps—the elder Sheehy had been an outstanding athlete with a promising career. He had had to choose between basketball and baseball, as the Minneapolis Lakers of the NBA and the Detroit Tigers of the American Baseball League wanted his talents. But neither received them. The Korean War broke out and the elder Sheehy gave his talents for his country. Now he is a bodyguard for Crown Prince Reza Pahlavi, son of the late Shah of Iran, who also attends Williams College.

"I was dedicated to being the best athlete I could be," remembers Harry. "I wanted the security that athletic success and recognition seemed to offer. My mother and father were divorced and I decided to find security in athletics as my family had not provided it. Others looked to good jobs, expensive cars, nice homes, or academic degrees—but I looked to athletics.

"I had a great deal of personal success at Williams. Yet it didn't seem to satisfy my friends, and I was greatly disillusioned to find that it didn't satisfy me. I found the life of an athlete to be very up and down. Our team was successful, but even this provided very little lasting satisfaction. People responded to me as an athlete on how well I played in my last game. I also realized that no matter how good I was, there was always someone better. So athletics failed me in my search for security."

Harry's search continued. He tried the party life; he tried meditation and Eastern religions; he tried anything that was available. He found weaknesses in all of them.

A young woman from Philadelphia, Connie Durrell, kept telling Harry where she had found security but he wouldn't listen. Sunday mornings Harry would be sleeping off the night before, only to be awakened in his dormitory by pounding on the door. It was Connie in her pretty Sunday dress trying to get him to go to church. Harry would tell her to get lost. Once, anticipating her arrival, he dumped water on her as she climbed the stairs.

"I had all the people who went to church in a neat little package," remembers Harry. "I was firmly convinced they were all a bunch of hypocrites. I told Connie that it just wasn't for me. If it was great for her, fine. But I wanted to be left alone—I didn't need it. She did say something, though, that I had never heard before and it stuck with me. She told me of a personal relationship with a living God through Jesus Christ."

Harry pursued a pro basketball career with even more zeal. But during the summer, he fell in a pick-up game and broke his wrist.

He suddenly realized how fragile and shaky the things are that most people depend upon for security. Everything could be taken away in an instant. Health, career, family, money, people—all prove to be rubber crutches. All are finite. All are worthwhile, but none are secure. None will last past the grave and some are destroyed before the grave.

"The broken wrist was the last straw," continues Harry. "I watched the other guys play and shot baskets by myself. They wouldn't let me play for fear I would hurt someone with my cast.

"There just had to be something or someone bigger than me in life, or anything else I could imagine. If there wasn't, life was pretty hopeless and didn't offer much reason for living. So that night I challenged God to be real in my life. I asked the Lord Jesus Christ to forgive my sins and show me security that was unshakeable. It was amazing—I had very little Bible knowledge at that point in my life, but I knew something had changed. I felt very peaceful and just knew of God's presence."

It was a whole year before Harry told anyone of his decision. He didn't want to tell anyone for fear of ridicule and rejection. He wouldn't even tell Connie —she had seen his involvement with many other things and would be skeptical. He was afraid she would think it was just another of his latest fads or security searches.

"Inwardly I was beginning to change," says Harry. "I still acted the way others expected me to, but I had a real sense of right and wrong that I had never had before. I was a real joker and would do anything to get laughs at other people's expense. I began to realize how much I was hurting these people. Finally, I told my younger sister, who is now also a Christian, and I told Connie. Her skepticism gave way to ecstasy.

"We even went to church together," laughs Harry.

In the spring of 1975, his senior year at Williams, Harry was invited to a try-out with the Athletes In Action basketball team in Indianapolis, Indiana. Coach Rle Nichols was impressed with his talents and offered him a spot on the team, a team devoted to spreading the gospel of Jesus Christ by playing basketball.

"It was a quality of life that I had never experienced before," recalls Harry. "A lot of my classmates were going on to graduate school to further their education and careers. But I was really attracted to this unique group of men in Indianapolis. Their faith was the focal point of their lives; it was an everyday experience. I wanted to be a part of it."

There were two AIA teams at that time: an eastern team based in Indiana and a western team based in Tustin, California. Harry played for the eastern team for two years and then rejected a pro offer from Portland of the NBA in favor of joining the western AIA team. He played there a year and then moved to Vancouver to join the Canadian team.

It had been decided to form two national teams, with the Indiana team moving to Canada and the California team representing the United States.

Harry is now a playing assistant coach to head coach Rle Nichols. He has seen tremendous growth and many changes.

"We play top university teams as well as international competition, including Russia and Yugoslavia. Being a Christian athlete is not an excuse to be second best. We are regarded as one of the top teams in Canada, recently splitting a series with the top-ranked, Jack Donahue-coached Canadian Olympic team. We are able to present the gospel to a segment of society that might otherwise not hear it. Most students on university campuses do not attend church, but they are exposed to the gospel when they attend our games. At many arenas we play in, there are people who have never heard the gospel. During halftime, we speak to the crowd about the wonderful news of the Lord Jesus Christ and challenge them to recognize Him as their Savior."

Reactions vary. Crowds can be noisy and obnoxious while they are speaking. At other times, you could hear a pin drop. Some opponents are openly hostile, not wanting to be beaten by a bunch of Bible thumpers. Some relish the competition.

"I remember one school we played where the fans reacted to every movement on the floor. They were avid basketball supporters. If you were playing for the home team, it was great—but being an opponent proved to be a little trying. At one point, their coach ran out on the floor, tore his coat off, and threw it over the bench. Soon the fans started throwing things, and during our halftime presentation, this type of disrespectful behavior continued.

"But we know that there is always someone listening, someone who has been searching. And suddenly, in a basketball arena, he hears the astounding good news. We often don't see the results as we travel extensively, but every once in a while someone will come up and say 'Thank you for introducing me to Jesus Christ.' Once after a church service, someone told us that a year earlier he had been at one of our games and had gone home and prayed to receive Jesus Christ. Whenever we get discouraged, God will bring someone forward whose life has been touched and changed by our ministry.

"It was a special thrill to play in Boston before my mother who had become a Christian," remembers Harry.

"Connie and I were married in 1977, and our lives are now spent spreading the gospel. We certainly do not have a problem-free or struggle-free life—**but** we do have a greater power source to deal with those struggles and problems, no matter how painful they may be. While we are happy, we are certainly not stagnant, and we constantly seek growth and development and change in our lives. Jesus Christ was the beginning of our lives, not the end. It's exciting to be able to tell people who are frustrated trying to find meaning and security in things that cannot possibly provide meaning and security, that peace and purpose and protection are all provided in one person only—the Lord Jesus Christ," says Harry.

At the end of each AIA basketball game, people are invited down to the floor to speak with the players. If you are searching for security, go and speak with Harry Sheehy. He was once where you are at and knows what it is like.

"My security doesn't depend on anything in this world," says Harry. "I don't know where I will be five or ten years from now, but I know Christ will be with me. If I die tomorrow, I know without a doubt where I will be—that is security!"

All men are like grass, and all their glory is like the flowers of the field. The grass withers and the flowers fall, but the word of our God stands forever. Isaiah 40:6b,8

8

Thousand-Point Kicker
Gerry Organ

Twelve-year-old Gerry Organ walked home with mixed feelings after a final soccer practice with his friends. Soccer was a major part of his life in his hometown of Cheltenham, about 100 miles northwest of London, England. He would miss all his soccer chums and wondered if there would be as much opportunity to play in Canada.

Gerry's young life was a comfortable compromise between school and soccer. But his father and grandfather had led a more rugged existence. His grandfather had been a sheepdrover. He had guided his flock from the English Cotswold countryside to market, a trip that took several days. Along with Gerry's dad, then just a lad, he slept in the open air by night and walked many miles by day.

Gerry's father also knew the meaning of hard work. He had joined the Royal Navy at the age of sixteen and served for 24 years, right through the second World War. But now he was restless and looking for new opportunity in Canada.

So the Organs settled in Toronto. Finding no lack of opportunity in his new home, Gerry immediately got involved in the only sport he knew and loved—soccer.

For the next ten years, spring, summer and fall were filled with practice and games and friendships with other soccer players. Gerry played for the Colts, Primo, Toronto City, Ukrainia, Kossuth Hungaria and for Canadian Kodak.

Then while in high school, Gerry got one of the first real shocks of his life.

"After four unspectacular years at York Memorial High School," Gerry remembers, "it was suggested by the principal that I go and get a job. This was a real blow to my comfortable life and my lifelong compromise of school and soccer came to a sudden halt!"

After working for four years, Gerry decided to go back to finish his final year of high school. "It's amazing what eight-hour days and $50 a week can do for one's motivation," Gerry says.

So he sold his '65 Volvo, went back to school and graduated the next year from Grade 13 at Scarlett Heights Collegiate. Then came plans for further education.

"Success, I was told, was achieved by obtaining a university education, securing a good job, finding a wife and settling down in a nice home in the country. Armed with this new insight and objective, I was accepted at the University of Guelph."

While at Guelph, Gerry met and married his wife, Lore (they both graduated in 1971 with bachelor of science degrees in physical education).

"Although neither of us were particularly religious, we never questioned our intention to marry in a church," Gerry says. "Lore had attended a Lutheran Church and had taught Sunday School and that's where we were married. My background was in the Anglican Church but throughout high school and university I had only occasional moments when I felt that I needed to deal with the issue of God.

"My occasional search for spiritual reality was hampered by the common concept that Jesus was just a good man of history and that God is some supreme abstract spirit that influences the fate of mankind," Gerry remembers. "My search generally ended in some nice feelings, but nothing else. No one had ever really explained to me the basics of Christian truth: 'that if you confess with your mouth Jesus as Lord, and believe in your heart that God raised Him from the dead, you shall be saved' " (Romans 10:9).

Because of his soccer background, Gerry had no trouble winning the kicking job for the university football team, the Guelph Gryphons. Coach Garney Henley, former Tiger Cat great, even taught him to play tight end as well as the basics of blocking and catching. But his transformation from a soccer player to a football player was not an easy one.

"When my number came up for 'Bull-In-The-Ring,' an insane football drill," Gerry remembers, "my then 180 pounds was literally crushed by Paul Zvonkin's 230. The greatest challenge in life at that time was climbing four flights of stairs at Johnston Hall after each practice."

Although Gerry was named to the first all-Canadian team in 1970, his university football career was anything but spectacular. So he wasn't surprised when he missed the college draft in the winter of 1971. He was making plans to attend graduate school at the University of Alberta when a classmate, Wilf Phillips, casually mentioned one day that he should pursue the possibility of playing in the CFL.

So Gerry swallowed his pride and wrote letters to five CFL teams, asking for a try-out. Frank Clair of the Ottawa Rough Riders was the only man to reply. Upon the recommendation of coaches Henley and Brown, Gerry was invited to training camp in 1971.

Some of the other teams now wish they had paid a little more attention to the English kicker. Kicking is the name of the game in Ottawa, and Gerry Organ puts the kick into the Rough Riders' game. A perennial points leader for the Eastern Football Conference Club, in an August 18, 1980, 33 to 11 win over the Alouettes, Organ kicked six field goals and scored 21 points to thrust his career total over the 1,000-point mark.

"I surprised everyone including myself at my first pro camp," remembers Gerry. "In the Black and White intrasquad game, I kicked three field goals and caught three passes for a total of 111 yards."

As a result, Gerry won the kicking job away from Ivan MacMillan. Since then Gerry's career awards have been numerous—he has been Eastern Football Conference scoring champion four times, the Schenley award winner for being the CFL's outstanding Canadian player, and in 1972 received three separate Most Valuable Player awards. The Riders always seem able to call on Gerry to produce crucial points and many times he has been called in to put the finishing touches on a football game. But he is not always successful.

"There's nothing you can do when you miss, especially when it ends up directly affecting the results of the game," says Gerry. "I've been zero for three and zero for four. It's pretty lonely. When it comes down to the crunch, there are six days a week when everybody wants to be a kicker and one day a week when nobody wants it.''

There have been last minute heroics though. Like the exciting game against Edmonton in 1977 when Gerry kicked a 51-yard field goal on the last play of the first half to give the Riders the lead. It was a terrific lift for the team to head to the locker room with that behind them—and equally devastating to the opposition. On the last play of the game, Gerry came in again to kick a 47-yard field goal to seal Edmonton's fate.

The 1976 Grey Cup game against Saskatchewan was indeed a classic. A Tommy Clements to Tony Gabriel pass late in the game secured the Ottawa victory and many felt it was the most exciting Grey Cup game for many years. In the third quarter, Gerry faked a punt and took off on a 52-yard run, hauled down by Saskatchewan's homegrown product and fellow Christian, Brian O'Hara, before crossing the goal line. The damage had been done though, and Ottawa went on to win the Grey Cup final.

Even though it was only an exhibition game, Gerry remembers one game against the Argos particularly well.

''We recovered no less than five onside kicks in the first half and led 21-0 before the Double-blue got a first down,'' Gerry remembers. ''My good friends Peter Muller and ''Big Z'' Andrusyshyn might not remember that game quite as well as I do.''

Besides Gerry's football career, life in general was successful for the Organs. Gerry and Lore had a beautiful country home and two wonderful children, Jamey and Leah. The search continued though, as all these things plus striving for fame and more money proved unsatisfying.

"In January of 1973, my 'Rider roommate,' Wayne Tosh, invited Lore and me to attend an Athletes in Action conference to be held in Miami," Gerry recalls. "Though unfamiliar with AIA, any reason to leave Ottawa and fly to Miami in January was good enough for me. As it turned out, we didn't enjoy our three days there. For the very first time we heard pros and their wives sharing their personal faith in Jesus Christ. Their message was so revolutionary that we decided that it wasn't for us and returned home somewhat disappointed but certainly enlightened.

"But at the start of the '73 season, I agreed to assist Wayne with a new program of pre-game devotionals for the players. At the fifth chapel, former hamilton Tiger Cat Paul Schmidlin was the speaker. The most amazing thing happened. I felt that Paul was speaking only to me!

"He shared that Jesus was either the true Son of God and our Lord and Savior, or indeed He was a liar and a lunatic. My preconceived notion of Jesus, just a good man, could not be considered. Given this choice and the evidence in my heart that I could not reject a Jesus who had died to set me free, I felt a compulsion and desire to set aside my intellectual hang-ups and by faith accept Jesus into my heart as my personal Savior and Lord. At the time, I had no real concept of the eternal consequences of this heart-felt step of faith."

Although Gerry's wife, Lore, accepted his new found faith, they did experience some difficulties relating to each other on spiritual matters. It was only after Lore accepted Jesus into her own life about six months later that the Organs began to discover how God intended a man and woman to share the joyful relationship of marriage.

"We have found that His unconditional love is sufficient to bind us together at the times when our natural love appears so weak and inadequate," Gerry says.

Gerry and Lore have also had many opportunities to talk about God's love from Newfoundland to British Columbia, giving them warm Christian friends right across the country. And now the Organs are looking forward to communicating their faith in a new way—through the medium of print.

"I'm excited about this book," says Gerry. "I'm believing God for great things. Someone who is searching for meaning in life, as I once did, will find the answer in these pages—fulfillment in life through Jesus Christ. There is a war going on for souls between God and the devil. Our short lifetime on earth is simply the opportunity for us to decide where we will spend eternity. The choice is ours and there is no middle ground."

For it is by grace you have been saved, through faith—and this not from yourselves, it is the gift of God—not by works, so that no one can boast. Ephesians 2:8,9a

PHOTOS

Left and above: NHL veteran Paul Henderson scored what many hockey buffs regard as the goal of the century—winning the first Canada-Russia series by slipping the puck past goalie Tretiak with only 34 seconds remaining in the final game. He is shown above with his wife, Eleanor, and their daughters, Heather, Jill, and Jennifer.

Overleaf: Kicker Zenon Andrusyshyn displays his talents for Toronto Argonaut fans in a regular season game against Hamilton, September 10, 1977. (Photo by Jerry Hobbs.)

Above: Playing for the Edmonton Eskimos, lineman Ron "Swamp Dawg" Estay was named Players' Association defensive lineman of the year, CFL All-Pro and Western Conference All-Star. He is shown here with his wife, Debbie, and their children, Brannon and Angela.

Above: Canadiens veteran Bernie "Boom Boom" Geoffrion, a member of the Hockey Hall of Fame, is one of hockey's all-time greats. The man who brought the slapshot to the NHL, the Boomer was the second player ever to score 50 goals in a season.

Gymnast Jennifer Diachun Palmer represented Canada in the 1968 and 1972 Olympics. She won a gold medal in the vault in the Cup of America championships, a gold medal on the balance beam at the South American Invitational, and was the 1974 Canadian National Champion in women's gymnastics.

Turning down an NBA offer, Harry Sheehy chose to play for the Athletes in Action Canadian basketball team and was named assistant playing coach. One of the top teams in Canada, the AIA squad uses halftime as an opportunity to tell about their Christian faith.

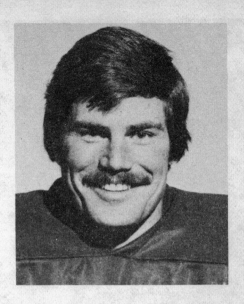

Above: Slotback and wide receiver Stu Lang has won the respect of fans and teammates alike. Nominated for the Schenley award in his rookie year with the Eskimos, Stu has also played in the CFL All-Star game and received the Canada Packer Award as Most Popular Player.

Left: Jim Hunter, shown here with his wife, Gail, is one of the greatest male skiers Canada has ever produced—five-time Canadian champion, World Professional Downhill champion, and top-ranked Olympic contender.

Above: Placekicker Gerry Organ was 1972's Most Valuable Player in the CFL, a Schenley award winner, and four-time Eastern Conference scoring champ. In a 1980 regular season game against the Montreal Alouettes, Gerry scored 21 points for the Ottawa Rough Riders, thrusting his career total over 1,000 points. (Photo above by Schwerdfeger Photography.)

Right: While with the Calgary Stampeders, defensive tackle John Helton won the Schenley award twice, was a perennial Western Conference All-Star and was named All-Canadian. He was traded to the Winnipeg Blue Bombers in 1978.

Above: Before becoming an NHL goalie with the Quebec Nordiques, Michel Dion was the World Hockey Association Ben Hatskin trophy winner for the best goals against average.

Left: Golfer Bill Tape won the Manitoba Open in 1974 and in 1975 edged out George Knudson on the final hole to become the Canadian PGA champion. (Photo by Hugh Allan.)

Left: Tight end Peter Muller, presently fourth on the Toronto Argonaut all-time pass reception list, is shown here in the Dacca, Bangladesh, home of Shohail Quamer, whom he has supported for a number of years. Peter visited the boy while on a four-month 1980 trip to the refugee camps of Thailand.

Above: Muller in an August 16, 1978, game against Edmonton in Exhibition Stadium, Toronto. (Photo by Rick Zarnett.)

Offensive guard Pat Bonnett was forced to take a year off active duty with the Montreal Alouettes because of a knee injury. He is shown here with his wife, Renee, their son, Aaron, and "miracle daughter" Trish. Trish was born with her spine not fully developed and lying outside her body, requiring emergency surgery.

NHL veteran Ron Ellis now has over 1,000 games and 330 goals under his belt. A highlight of his career was the first Canada-Russia series—he was a forward on one of the more successful lines with Paul Henderson and Bobby Clarke. He is shown above with his wife, Jan, and their children, R.J. and Kitty. (Left photo courtesy the **Toronto Sun.**)

Jean Pronovost began his NHL career in 1968 with the Pittsburgh Penguins. In the 1975-76 season, he scored 52 goals and made 52 assists for a total of 104 points. He was traded to the Atlanta Flames in 1978 and in 1980 went to the Washington Capitals.

9

A Complete Man
Stu Lang

The Canadian Football League Players' Association was on strike in the spring of 1972. But the Edmonton Eskimos' training camp was a beehive of activity, buzzing with rookies delighted with the extra time the strike afforded them to show their talents to the coaches.

With no veterans to overshadow them, they paraded their skills and enthusiasm before the critical eyes of head coach Ray Jauch and his staff. They were all there to prove one thing: they were worthy of wearing the Green and Gold.

The intense demands of the twice-a-day drills and the long hours of watching films and learning play assignments were gruelling. Pressure and tension grew daily as many men fought for few jobs. The coaching staff vented their frustration with the veterans' strike by the physical demands they made on the rookies. But finally the nightly team meeting was over and final preparations had been discussed for the first exhibition game of the season. The recruits would be tested under game conditions against the British Columbia Lions.

Coach Jauch dismissed the group early so they

could relax and enjoy those cherished hours prior to curfew.

"Lang," his voice cracked the air. "I'd like to speak with you."

Rookie Stu Lang, recently of the Queen's University Golden Gaels, felt his heart skip and his stomach knot.

"I hear you broke curfew last night. You won't be making the trip with the rest of us."

"I was shocked," states Lang. "My jaw almost hit the floor."

Suddenly a wide smile broke over Jauch's face, "You won't be making the trip because we think you've got a real good shot at making this club. We've seen enough and want you to stay behind and work with the veterans. The strike is over."

It was the beginning of a long and close relationship of mutual respect and admiration between coach and player.

Though given a shot of confidence, Lang was gently reminded of his rookie status. Used footballs rate higher than a rookie in training camp. Veterans see the newcomers as prima donnas threatening someone's job. They are the object of humor, practical jokes and scare tactics. Coaches, trainers, equipment people…all take part in the annual ritual. Rookies are to be seen, not heard—and the sooner they realize it and let their skills do their talking for them, the better off they are.

"I had a real advantage though," states Stu. "My former teammate and captain at Queen's was Mike Lambros who was now a veteran, and my locker was beside veteran Gary Lefevbre who was really open and friendly."

Fortunate is the rookie who is taken under the wing

of a veteran during the doubts and trials of the pressure cooker known as training camp. A little encouragement and advice at the right time and place can go a long way in his making or not making the team.

Not that Lang needed any help. The 6'1", 190 lb. athlete had an impressive record. He had played two varsity sports while at Queen's—hockey and football. As a high school student he had played both sports as well as rugger and track at long established and respected Upper Canada College in the heart of Toronto.

Reflecting back on those days, he says, "I was excited about the lifestyle and prominence of pro athletes. We'd go down to Maple Leaf Gardens or the Canadian National Exhibition to watch the Leafs and Argos. I wanted to play pro sports but did not know which sport to choose. It wasn't until I was at Queen's that I decided that football was my greatest area of achievement."

But it was while he was playing hockey at Upper Canada College that he was nicknamed "Swoop," attempting to mimic the smooth-skating NHL star, Frank Mahovlich.

To date, Stu has put in seven years as a slotback and wide receiver with the mighty Grey Cup champion Eskimos, but he still vividly remembers his first pro game: "We were playing the Ottawa Rough Riders. I was pacing back and forth in the halls of the dorm, concentrating on my play assignments and preparing myself mentally for the game. Mike Lambros passed me and invited me to pre-game chapel. I really wasn't interested in going, but then he told me it was open to everyone and the coaches would be there. I figured it would be a good time to get some brownie points—'Hey, look at Stuie Lang, a real team man; he even goes to chapel.'

"The speaker that day talked about the concept of the complete or whole man—physical, intellectual and spiritual. All of a sudden the truth hit home. Everything made sense. It was just like a light going on in a dark room. I realized I had no spiritual dimension in my life."

As a baby, Stu could not walk and had little strength. Yet he now earned his living as a professional athlete—his physical life was surely developed! As a child he could not read or write. But now he was a graduate of one of Canada's most respected universities with a degree in chemical engineering—his intellectual life was surely developed! But there had never been any spiritual awareness or growth!

"Church had always been a social thing for me. I thought I was a Christian by the things I did, yet there was never any reality or application of Christian principles in my life. My main reason for going to church was to qualify for their hockey team, and every Sunday we had a mini hot-stove session out in the area where the coats were hung. We would go over the Leafs' exploits of the past week. There was nothing solid in my life and I just drifted away from church. I had always heard a lot **about** Jesus Christ, but I didn't know Him as this chapel speaker seemed to. It was just like I knew a lot about the Leafs, but I had never met any of them. He challenged me to invite Jesus Christ into my life as my Lord and Savior and enter into a personal relationship with Him. In other words, begin a spiritual dimension as well as physical and intellectual...complete my development as a total person. It just seemed like the most natural and sensible thing in the world to do.''

It wasn't the first time that Stu had heard the gospel, but it was the first time he understood his need.

"God had always been sort of a rabbit's foot to me. I'd ask Him for help to score a hat trick or a touchdown, or for a win or to stay injury-free.''

While at Upper Canada College, he met fellow student Barry Petit who belonged to the same intramural division within the school—Mowbray's House. ''Barry was the first person whom I had ever met whose faith seemed real. His standard of belief was the Bible, and he lived according to its teaching. He was really unique as far as I was concerned, but I felt no desire then to adopt his way of life.''

Neither one could ever, in his wildest dreams, imagine the surprise that was in store for them years ahead.

Stu began to work hard on developing his new-found wholeness. He continued to practice his football skills, setting a sound foundation for a successful CFL future. His dedication and discipline on and off the field gained him the respect of teammates, fans and the media. Nominated for the Schenley award for top rookie in the CFL, Stu has also played in the CFL All-Star game and received the Canada Packer Award as Most Popular Player.

Off the field, he began to study the work of historians and Bible scholars, seeking to explore and support his faith. He began to read the Bible and pray. He had learned his lesson well as an athlete: master the fundamentals and you have mastered the game. Fundamentals are similar to and as important as taking a shower. It's not enough to take one on

Sunday and hope you will stay clean the rest of the week; you take one every day! You don't work on your fundamentals once a week and hope you will improve. You practice them every day. He began to grow!

"It was very frustrating as I tried to share my joy with my old school friends who were very close to me. I wanted them to have what I had. After our first game in Toronto against the Argos, we all got together and I excitedly told them what had happened in my life, only to be met by a barrage of intellectual arguments. Their attitude seemed to be, 'When I see it, I'll believe it,' whereas I tried to explain to them, 'When you believe it, you will see it.' No one has to kiss his brains good-bye to believe in the historical and theological facts of Jesus Christ. The harder you search, the more you believe. The more you believe, the sooner you will come face to face with the greatest intellectual who has ever lived, and almost 2,000 years later is still living—Jesus Christ."

Stu's future wife, Kim, was living in Toronto prior their marriage. She was also a Queen's graduate and was completing work on a second degree at the Ontario Teacher Education College.

"I thought he was involved in some kind of cult," she recalls, "but gradually as I met other Christian ballplayers and saw more of Stu, I realized I saw something I hadn't seen in him before. I began to evaluate my own spiritual life and I too became a Christian. We're both very thankful that we have Jesus Christ as the focal point of our marriage."

Stu and Peter Muller of the Argos share a special concern for their respective families. "Peter and I attended John Ross public school together in

Toronto. Although we went our separate ways, I followed his career and was in the stands as a Queen's student, watching him play in his first Blue-White intrasquad game. We both love our families very much and we want them to know the fulness of the Lord Jesus Christ in their lives. We regularly pray for each other's family.''

Stu was given his first public opportunity to declare his stand for Christ following the Grey Cup game in Vancouver in 1974.

''I was speaking one morning in a local church and when I looked up, there in the front row was Barry Petit, my old friend from Upper Canada College, who was visiting in Vancouver. I just couldn't believe it! Barry came up to me afterward and told me how he had been praying that I would become a Christian ever since that day when he had shared the gospel with me. He thought he was there to visit only; instead he witnessed my first public declaration of Jesus Christ. We were both so excited and surprised we could hardly talk.''

Do you believe in coincidence, Stu?

''No, I believe in God!''

For the message of the cross is foolishness to those who are perishing, but to us who are being saved it is the power of God. For it is written: 'I will destroy the wisdom of the wise; the intelligence of the intelligent I will frustrate.' Where is the wise man? Where is the scholar? Where is the philosopher of this age? Has not God made foolish the wisdom of this world? For since in the wisdom of God the world through its wisdom did not know Him, God was pleased through the foolishness of what was preached to save those who believe.

I Corinthians 1:18-21

10

Downhill Explosion
Jim Hunter

"It was the spring of 1963, and I was ten years old. My younger brother, Lorne, and I were jumping on my bed in the basement of our farm house in Shaunavon, Saskatchewan. We were trying little half-flips and landing on our behinds. It was fun, if not too great for the bed. Then one of us got the bright idea to try a back flip. Naturally, I had to try it first. Instead of jumping straight up like I should have, though, I jumped backwards. When I came down, the flip was only half done. I landed on the iron bar at the end of the bed, fell to the floor, and cracked the back of my head on the cement. Everything went black."

Jungle Jim Hunter, future Canadian National Alpine Ski Champion, lay in a coma for three days. He crushed his skull in the fall and had to wear a special protective helmet for three months after the accident. As he suffered from memory lapses, his schoolwork was greatly affected. Branded abnormal by teachers, he was assumed academically inferior and placed in a slow learners class. Classmates made fun of his helmet.

"I was treated like I never wanted to be treated

again," says Jim. "I had to prove I wasn't an idiot. I had to be a winner at something. I loved to compete, and I concentrated all my competitiveness on sports."

Jim Hunter knows two speeds: fast and stop. There is no in-between.

"Dad always made sure we had a place to skate. At first, he leveled off some ground and, when the weather got cold enough, he watered it. But it seemed like each year he added something. Before long we had a regulation-sized rink there on the farm. It had boards, lines, nets, everything. In Saskatchewan, the winter sun can disappear as early as three o'clock in the afternoon. After school was out, we would drive the car and the half-ton pickup to opposite corners of the rink and aim the headlights onto the ice. On winter mornings, we'd skate over to the barn, slip on the skate guards, milk the 76 cows, take off the skate guards and skate back to the kitchen for breakfast.

"We filled old cement bags with 20 pounds of sand and put them on chairs. After pushing them ten or twenty times up and down the ice in the afternoon, we would go and milk the cows again. We practiced with steel pucks to strengthen our shooting, passing and handling. During the summers, we spent up to five weeks at hockey camps across Canada. Looking for better competition, my mom, my brother and I moved to Calgary, while my dad and sister, Marilyn, stayed on the farm. Almost every week-end my mom would make the 600-mile round trip to see Dad and Marilyn."

If determination, grit and hard work were all it took to make dreams come true, all three of Lloyd Hunter's boys would have become professional hockey players.

There was a spiritual side to Jim Hunter as well. Listening to a missionary speaker at the age of eight, Jim's adventuresome spirit was captured by the stories of spreading the gospel in foreign countries. He decided he wanted to be a missionary.

While the missionary packed up all his curios, Jim crawled into the back seat of the car and lay down on the floor. The missionary finished saying good-byes, packed his materials in the trunk and climbed behind the wheel. He didn't notice the sleeping boy until the car hit a bump and a tired but excited Jim Hunter said, "What mission field are we going to?" The missionary returned his stowaway to the church.

But the missionary had made a lasting impression. Jim was convicted when the missionary spoke of the punishment for sin. He had stolen money from his father's dresser, and had been caught slipping jawbreakers into his sleeve down at the local store. Jim asked Jesus Christ to forgive his sins.

At the age of eleven, Jim discovered skiing. The man who would someday ski the great mountains of Japan, Austria, Switzerland, Italy, France and Chile started skiing in the ditches of Saskatchewan.

"We grew tired of being pulled around behind a horse, so Dad drove the pick-up truck and we'd take turns holding onto the 40-foot rope attached to the rear bumper. Dad drove along the roads and we skied on the deep snow in the ditches. We'd run into a snow drift, the rope would yank taut, and we'd explode out of the drift into the air. We'd pull around to the side of the truck like a water skier, just missing the telephone poles along the road. Then we'd cut back across, catch a drift, and jump over the road and land on the other side.''

When he wasn't playing hockey in Calgary, Jim had a choice between ballet and skiing. He chose to ski and soon attracted the attention of the Calgary Skimeisters, a club that promoted ski racing and helped young racers. Jim began to enjoy skiing more and more. He loved the individual recognition—not having to share the credit or blame with anyone but himself. Summer hockey camps were replaced with summer ski camps.

Jim didn't make many friends in Calgary so went to great lengths to impress his classmates and teachers.

''I often wore a suit and tie to school, and I usually carried a briefcase with my Bible inside. It was my immature and superficial way of showing people I was a Christian. I wanted people to see I was different. I may not have succeeded in communicating my faith effectively, but my goal of being noticed was a huge success.''

Jim was different. He was a country kid, a religious nut, a show-off. He thrived on being different. He would stay after school reading or toying with the piano. He would tell his parents he was doing extra work. The real reason was that he was waiting for the class bullies to leave. They would wait for him at the bike rack to ridicule him and shove him around. They were jealous of his being the only male member of the Glee Club chorus. He dreaded facing them.

Later, Jim attended Kokanee Glacier Camp sponsored by the Canadian National Ski Team. It was an intensive period of training and teaching. He thrived on it—he had prepared for it. His dad had bought him 300 lbs. of weights and he lifted them as the wall charts indicated. He drank gallons of protein supplement. He ran miles behind the tractor and the cultivator in the fields. Inspired by Canada's ski queen, Nancy Greene, he did daily push-ups and sit-ups and skipped rope. He strove to do 85 push-ups in a minute. through a skillful blend of intimidation, encouragement and example, his trainers convinced him that skiing was an explosion down a hill. Nothing else mattered but speed. He had everything it took to be a champion—except humility.

Jim was also the religious kid, the one who said it was wrong to swear and tell dirty jokes. He would be the brunt of ridicule as he read his Bible at night while others directed questions at him about sex. Laughed at while trying to recapture his Bible that was being thrown around the room, he cried in total isolation when his beloved Bible was thrown into the roaring flames of the wood burning stove. He wasn't able to replace it.

He took his sleeping bag outside and slept on the mountain. He prayed, "Lord, make me a winner so I can prove You are real."

"Skiing could actually be my means of serving God—I could ski for God's glory," remembers Jim. "I was convinced that I was destined to win. I had to. If I was skiing for God, then I needed to win so He could be honored by my victories, and I would be respected when I told others about my beliefs. In my teenage mind, God was now going to take over and bring success. In a strange twist, turning my skiing into my mission increased the pressure. Skiing took on eternal dimensions. Losing became not just a disappointment, but a disgrace to God. Skiing to me was no longer a sport—it was holy war."

Jim wrote Al Raine, the alpine director of the Canadian Ski Association, **telling** him he was good enough for the national team. He trained harder.

"I was running ten miles each morning, doing 80 one-armed push-ups every day, lifting weights and riding distances on my bicycle. I discovered I could hang from a door by my toes. It wasn't a stunt; it was a great way to strengthen the toes and lower leg," recalls Jim.

He aimed for the Olympics, then two years away. He was 16 years old.

He made the B squad of the National team and competed on the international circuit. He trained harder.

"Even the day before a race, I'd be up at 6:00 a.m. to run two miles, do 50 push-ups, 100 sit-ups and 100 rope skips. After the race, I'd repeat the work-out," says Jim.

At the end of the season, he was not only on the A team, but was Canada's best hope to win World Cup points and an Olympic medal the next year in Sapporo, Japan. He reacted to the new pressure the only way he knew how—he trained harder.

"Back on the farm in Shaunavon, Dad and I devised a whole conditioning program tailored to the farm setting. Each morning, I continued to do my push-ups, rope skipping and running. I practiced slalom technique by setting up a series of old tires and jumping side-to-side from one to the next. If I touched the tires with either of my feet, I made myself do 50 push-ups. In addition, while I was driving the tractor, I discovered ways to train from behind the wheel. I did my sit-ups on the seat of the tractor as I drove. After that I stood on the seat and practiced my pre-jumps—tucked in a racing crouch,

I'd leap as high as I could, bring my knees up to my chest, and return to the tractor seat in my tuck. I'd do that as many times as I could before the tractor needed a steering correction.

"Sometime during the middle of the summer, I read a magazine article explaining how astronauts were spun around in sophisticated modules to train them to keep their balance in a weightless environment. I mentioned it to Dad, and it inspired another of his brainstorms. We didn't have sophisticated equipment, but we did have a huge tractor with wheels large enough to crawl into, and if being spun around could give astronauts a better sense of balance, why shouldn't it work for skiers?

"So we gathered a couple of old pillows and wedged me inside the rim of the tractor tire, while Dad got in the cab. He drove around in tight circles for two or three minutes. I had my head between my knees, so I didn't see much while Dad was driving. When the tractor stopped, I crawled out and tried to get into a racing crouch. The world kept spinning, and I couldn't keep up with it. I tumbled over. My body refused to remain upright.

"I kept extensive notes on everything I could think of—what I ate, my pulse rate, the hours I slept, the miles I ran, the exercises I did, and the various wax combinations that work best on different kinds of snow. I drew diagrams of the various World Cup courses and how to get down them the quickest. I was also reading the Bible daily and taking notes on what I thought about it. Most of those journal entries repeated my determination to win so that God would be honored."

Only three Canadian male skiers had qualified for the Olympics—Reto Barrington, Derek Robbins and

Jim. He felt it was an absolute necessity for him to win.

"Lord, if You want people to listen to me when I tell them about You, You've got to make me a winner," prayed Jim. He finished 20th in the downhill, and although it was the best finish a Canadian had ever made in Olympic competition, to Jim it was worthless. "I felt I had let down my team, my country and my God," says Jim.

He made up for the downhill disaster with an 11th place giant slalom finish. Only one event remained, the slalom. Jim finished 21st.

"The Olympics were over for me," remembers Jim. "I hung around the Olympic village, sightseeing and waiting for the closing ceremonies. Then I got the surprise of my life. When they announced the results of the combined alpine events, I had finished third behind Walter Tresch and Gustavo Thoeni. I had won a bronze medal in Olympic competition. For an eighteen-year-old, I figured this was a good start. I was on my way. My formula was working."

Jim's career rapidly progressed. He was introduced to the World Cup races and the fanatical, European racing crowds. He walked up a giant slalom course on his skis, over a mile and a half, to study the run and also for psych purposes. Other skiers laughed at him.

Jim laughed last.

A racer from the second seed, Jim Hunter, number 28, won the first run of the giant slalom. It was almost unheard of—the spectators went crazy. He was just one good run away from a World Cup race. Under pressure, he climbed the hill a second time with his skis on. He knew he could prove himself.

The snide comments, his brashness, his lifestyle, his religion, his training—all would be recognized if he won the second run. "Lord, make me a winner," Jim prayed.

Halfway down the hill, it seemed his prayer would be answered. Over the loudspeaker, he heard it announced in Italian that his midway time was a full second ahead of the fastest competitor.

"But as I skidded around the third last turn, my legs got too far apart, my outside ski slipped, and I felt myself losing my balance. Frantically I dug in, but the rocks didn't allow my edges to catch. I was still on my feet and barely made it past the next gate. But now I had to shift my weight to turn the other direction. It was steep, and my ski slipping caused me to slide too low. I tried to collect myself but the skis let go again. My feet went out from under me.

"There was total silence. It was like the world had ended. I was out of the race. At that moment, I didn't have any desire to ski again. I knew I'd had my chance to win, and I'd missed it."

The workhorse champion had many more chances. He traveled all over the world and competed against the world's best skiers. He would become the five-time Canadian champion. He would become one of the greatest male skiers Canada has ever produced. He would become the World Professional Downhill Champ. He would suffer many injuries and he would continue to train harder.

In 1976, in Innsbruck, Austria, the European papers heralded him as the expected Olympic champion. But during a practice run at 50 mph, thinking only of Olympic gold, he did not see the German spectator until it was too late. Snow, skis and bodies flew into the air. Jim passed over the tails of the spectator's skis and hit him solidly in the back with his left shoulder. In shock, four years of Olympic adrenalin drained quickly from his body. Only a few hours later, Hunter, the pre-race favorite, was able to muster only a 10th place finish!

He didn't have a close friend to his name. He didn't get along with newsmen or his teammates. His selfish ambition drove others away.

In Zurich, he ran down the stairs of a cheap hotel crying. A teammate had thrown his Bible out the window and it landed among the prostitutes. He ran by the canal and prayed, "Lord, make me a winner if You want people to listen to me when I tell them about You." After the others had gone to sleep, he returned and silently did 100 push-ups and 100 sit-ups and went to sleep.

But today there is a new Jim Hunter.

"I've finally seen that my winning isn't as important to God as letting other people see the love of God in my life. Yes, I'm still a skier, and want to win, but a new goal is now in my mind: to introduce other people to Christ. My arrogance and selfishness did nothing to accomplish this goal. My Christianity is to be revealed in my love for others, not in winning ski races," says Jim.

He and his wife, Gail, are very active in Christian work. They have participated in Billy Graham crusades, and work at their goal of sharing Christ's love by speaking to churches, retreats and youth groups. They show ski films and share that while skiing is important, Jesus Christ is more important.

"It's a lesson that I should have learned long ago but didn't. God doesn't necessarily ask us to be successful, He asks us to be faithful. He doesn't use winners all the time, He uses people who say, 'Here

I am Lord, I'm available.' Knowing that God accepts us in spite of our failures, we don't need to hide them or fear them. I'm finally beginning to see progress over that mountain of impatience, short temper and arrogance. I haven't conquered the peak, by any means, but I've made visible progress. Sensing that slow, sometimes almost imperceptible change in my personality was the most profound victory in my life."

Now peaceful, Jim Hunter is a real winner!

All men will know that you are my disciples if you love one another.   John 13:35

11

Traded!
John Helton

There were rumors in the air. It was February 1978 and defensive tackle John Helton, 6'2'', 250 lbs., had not yet signed a contract with the Calgary Stampeders. Negotiations were at a standstill.

In the meantime, he was putting in a normal day at his off-season job, selling advertising at radio station CFCN.

In his ten years at the Calgary club, the 31-year-old veteran had earned impressive credentials. He was a perennial Western Conference All-Star, had won the coveted Schenley award twice, and had been named All-Canadian.

But now it looked as though his Calgary career could be over.

"I had an agent negotiating for me. I didn't feel it was right for me as a player to be directly involved with my head coach and general manager Jack Gotta. In the locker room, I thought, he's going to tell me I'm an excellent football player. But in the office, he'll say I'm not good enough to get the amount of money for the level of excellence that he told me in the locker room I've achieved. That kind of situation can only lead to friction and it's best handled by a third party, an agent.''

But in this case, the agent complicated the situation rather than simplifying it. He did not reside in Calgary and could not meet with the club directly. The Stampeders seemed to be in no rush to sign John; they certainly were not knocking any doors down to get to him. Perhaps their minds were already made up. Perhaps they felt John's career was washed up. Perhaps they felt his usefulness was finished.

Club directors and those close to the team professed to know nothing. While they thought highly of John Helton the man, they knew they would have to trust in the judgment of the man they had hired to solve such matters—the general manager.

The press seemed to be as much in the dark as anyone else about John Helton's future. They weren't negative toward John—but they weren't positive either. When a businessman has a bad day at work, few outside his immediate influence are aware of it. But when an athlete has a bad day on the field, he and the rest of the country can read about it in the morning paper.

But John wasn't too upset.

''Whether I would be playing football in the CFL or the NFL was the only question in my mind,'' says John. ''The rookies were just learning the skills I had, and I could still perform them as well as, or better than, any veteran.''

As far as John was concerned, he knew what he would be doing. But he didn't know where.

John Helton had enjoyed and benefited from his time in Calgary. And Calgary enjoyed and benefited from having John play for them. It all started when

130

the Arizona State University graduate listened to the opinions of Stampeders Herman Harrison, Bob Lueck and Rick Shaw.

"They had all played at Arizona State and when they returned at Christmas they always spoke real well of the Calgary club," John remembers. "I had always wanted to play in a small metropolitan area—I had been thinking of the Green Bay Packers. Then when I wasn't drafted by the Buffalo Bills of the NFL until the sixth round, Calgary looked pretty appealing."

That initial interest led to a 10-year Calgary career. In that time, he missed only three games. Many times he played against medical advice. On game days he ran on ankles that during the preceding week were too swollen to walk on. A defensive lineman must react quickly to opposition ball carriers while trying to prevent being blocked out of the play by skilled and strong offensive linemen. John reacted for years on knees that were twisted, with shoulders that had been strained, and with a neck that had often been jammed. Professional ball carriers are agile, elusive and forceful. A tackler uses many parts of his body to stop him—but he has to use his hands. Many times John grabbed and hung on with fingers that were jammed and swollen and sprained. But he accepted the pain. It was part of the game.

As a professional, he realized his contract negotiations were part of the game as well.

"I had seen it happen to a lot of other guys, and I figured it would eventually happen to me as well. I didn't expect any help and I didn't get any. So I released the agent and let time take care of things. I was happy to have been able to contribute for as long as I did.

"I knew I wanted to continue to play football, though. My relationship to football was like a fish to water—that was my home, my environment. I had no bitter feelings towards the club; I had been around long enough to know how these things went. But my peace of mind came from knowing that God was simply pointing me in another direction and was going to use the Stampeders to show me the way.

"There are times when I tell my children to do something for their own good. They may not want to or understand why at the time, but they trust me as their father. God is my heavenly Father. I became an adopted son when I asked Jesus Christ to be my Savior. I may not know why things happen, but I trust in Him. There are no mistakes and accidents in life. Anything that happens has been allowed to happen by God. If God allows things to happen in my life, no matter what the circumstances, I know it must be for my own good. I wouldn't allow anything to happen to my children that would harm them, and God has a lot more love than I do," states John.

"I'm almost embarrassed to admit how I once thought of my relationship to God. As a football player, I was rated and tested weekly. I·was used to being graded. Game charts and films showed not only my strengths, but my weaknesses as well. In the same way, I knew I hadn't given Christ very much in my life, so I sincerely thought I was too far gone. I believed in God—on road trips I read the Bible the Gideons put in the hotel rooms. But I just figured I'd live my life out, do the best I could and hope for the best when I died."

But something happened to change all that.

"We were playing the 1974 All-Star Game in

Ottawa, and during the pre-game chapel I heard this incredible message," he recalls. "I was told of the gospel of Jesus Christ, that Jesus Christ came to save sinners. To be saved, all you had to do was ask to be saved. Well, I sure knew I was a sinner, but I was astounded. How could it be that easy?

"But that was all the hope I needed to hear—I raised my hand way up high to make sure God saw me and I prayed right then and there to ask the Lord Jesus Christ to forgive my sins. Then I read in the Bible that when Christ forgave my sins, I became His brother. That means we have the same Father—God! Now I'm constantly trying to show the Lord how grateful I am.

"As an athlete, there are times you are taken advantage of and you resent it; you feel used. As a Christian, nothing is more exciting than to be used by the Lord Jesus Christ. To be able to serve Him is a privilege, not a job."

The phone rang in the radio sales office. It was John's wife, Nora. They had known each other since grade one back in Mt. Union, Pennsylvania.

"Nora read me the letter she received from the Stampeders. It was the usual good-bye. They told me I had been a credit to the community, a fine football player. But now I was the property of the Winnipeg Blue Bombers. I no sooner got off the phone with Nora than there was a message to call Winnipeg. Coach Jauch left the meetings they were having during the press conference to welcome me to the club. We both looked forward to completing negotiations as quickly as possible."

The Heltons wrapped up their business commitments and holidayed in Phoenix, Arizona. By the time they returned to Calgary, it was time for John to head for Winnipeg to get ready for training camp and find a new home. Nora and the kids stayed behind so the school year would not be disrupted.

As a Stampeder, tens of thousands had cheered the exploits of John Helton. One incident die-hard fans won't forget is the time Saskatchewan's legendary quarterback, Ron Lancaster, threw a screen pass out to the flat in a 1974 game. Nothing unusual about that, you say—Lancaster has thrown millions of them. Yes, but in this instance, a pursuing defensive tackle by the name of John Helton had been fooled by Lancaster. John forgot about Lancaster and quickly turned downfield in pursuit of the pass receiver. He pulled him down on the 5-yard line after a 50-yard chase. Lancaster ran the next two plays up the middle, and each time the ball carrier ran into John Helton. Frustrated, Lancaster had to settle for a field goal attempt on the last down. What had looked like a certain touchdown had been snuffed by John Helton. Thousands roared their approval and appreciation.

The day John left Calgary, six people showed up to bid him farewell: Nora, his three children—Jessica, Jason and Justin—and two close friends, Margaret Keeley and Lacci Maharaj.

"It was time to leave," says John. "The Lord had a job for me to do in Winnipeg."

Playing for the Blue Bombers, John was nominated for the Schenley. Voted in by the men he works against, the offensive linemen throughout the league, John was also the proud recipient of the Mack Truck Award as the top defensive lineman in the CFL.

"I don't have all the answers, and there are times

when I get upset with my problems, the same way anyone does. I know I'll never be without problems in life, but I'll never be without Christ either. Even when I forget Him and let my problems affect me, He doesn't forget me. He's only too willing for me to hand them over to Him. Being cut or traded is a traumatic experience to a lot of athletes. It can be a tremendous shock to somebody's ego. If you consider that your status in life is determined by football, when your football career is affected, you will be affected as well. But my status in life is determined by my relationship to Christ. In addition to all the other positive things that were produced in the trade, I was given a deeper trust in my relationship to Christ.

"Without Jesus Christ I'd be hopelessly lost," concludes a thankful Winnipeg Blue Bomber—John Helton.

And the peace of God, which transcends all understanding, will guard your hearts and your minds in Christ Jesus. Philippians 4:7

12

A Natural Kind of Life
Jean Pronovost

Two Atlanta Flames' hockey players, Jean Pronovost and Don Bouchard, sat in a hotel coffee shop in New York City. They were having coffee and killing time preparing for the game that night against the Rangers. It was a way of life for Pronovost, the high scoring veteran NHL right-winger. He had joined Atlanta after ten years with the Pittsburgh Penguins. The major topic of discussion was teammate Ed Kea.

"I had played against Ed Kea when I was with Pittsburgh," recalls Jean. "Prior to coming to Atlanta, I had met him in Los Angeles before a game. Pittsburgh flew in the same night Atlanta and the Kings were playing. Atlanta was staying in the same hotel we were in, and I had coffee with Ed. I really envied and was curious about the peace of mind that Ed always seemed to have. Now that we were both playing for Atlanta, I got a real close look at how he handled the pressures of the game and how he dealt with his injuries."

Jean was having a trying year with a nagging knee injury. In his previous two seasons, he had scored 52 and 40 goals respectively with the Penguins.

Recovering from his knee injury, he constantly found himself struggling and two steps behind the play. It was natural for him to watch how Kea coped with adversity.

But Jean was leery about Ed Kea. He was aware of the talk around the league.

"I knew that Ed was a born-again Christian," says Jean. "I heard they were all a bunch of fanatics and Jesus freaks. Some of the guys thought they were some kind of cult or something. I was curious to know more. But I just didn't want anyone to associate me with that kind of thing. Regardless, everybody seemed to respect Ed Kea."

At the same time, Jean had been noticing a lot of changes at home as well. His wife, Diane, was like a new woman. Their two sons, Eric, 11, and Marty, 8, had also noticed the change.

"I remember playing Junior "A" with the Niagara Falls Flyers," says Jean. "Our first year I was the top scorer and we won the Memorial Cup. My only goal in life was to be a pro hockey player. I idolized my older brother Marcel who played with Detroit and Toronto. I thought it was the best life anyone could ever want.

"Well, that first summer back home, I met Diane at a baseball game in our hometown of Beauharnois, Quebec. I spent so much time courting her that I didn't train very much. I returned to Niagara Falls out of shape. We were playing the Junior Canadiens early in the season and Serge Savard caught me with my head down—I separated my shoulder and pinched a nerve in my back.

"Diane and I got married, and after two years in Oklahoma City and eleven years in the NHL, she was used to being a hockey wife. There were a lot of

things she didn't like, but she made the best of it.
But when she asked me if she could go to a Bible
study with some of the other hockey, football and
baseball wives, I told her to stay away from that kind
of stuff. People were going to think she was crazy. I
told her to start playing tennis or taking classes at
the university if she was bored.

"I really noticed two areas about her, though. She
always used to be after me to buy things. Now when
I would tell her to go buy something, she would tell
me it was too expensive or that we didn't need it.
Also, I really used to bug her by sleeping late in the
morning. She would bang the doors, vacuum—anything to make noise and make me get up. Lately,
though, it was really quiet and I started to feel
guilty. One morning I went down expecting to get a
blast and I got a big kiss and 'I love you.' My breakfast was all ready. It really boggled my mind,''
remembers Jean.

Diane laughs and remembers how scared she was
to tell Jean she was not only attending Bible studies
secretly, but had also asked the Lord Jesus Christ to
forgive her sins and come into her life.

"I didn't go to the Bible study the first time the
girls asked,'' she says. "But Jennifer Kea, Robin
Plett, Sarah Shand and I belonged to the same car
pool. On the way to the Omni, they would talk about
what they were learning at Bible study. I was concerned at the time about our two boys. We hadn't been
church-goers for awhile and the boys weren't
receiving any instruction at all. Also, I was really
scared of being left alone—not only because Jean
was on the road, but because divorce is so common
in pro sports. If Jean had ever left me, I would have
had no skills or career to fall back on. I was the oldest

wife on the team, but the other girls were telling me how they were learning to be better wives.

"So I decided to go to their Bible study. After attending a few times, I was really excited but also very scared. It was so different from my previous experiences with religion and so much more fulfilling. Penny Nossette, the leader, kept asking me to go for lunch, but I was reluctant. Finally I suggested we go to a little French restaurant in Atlanta. I couldn't take it anymore. I just had to find out what a born-again Christian was as I was so confused.

"I was just astonished when Penny showed me in the Bible that I didn't have to be afraid of death, that I could be assured of eternal life, and most important, that the Lord Jesus Christ promised to never leave me once I believed in Him and asked Him to be my Savior.

"Jean was on the road, so I rushed home to share my excitement with the boys. I prayed that night to ask the Lord Jesus Christ to forgive me. I always used to have trouble sleeping when Jean was away, but that night I slept so well; I had such a sense of peace. I run every day, and when running the next morning, I felt like I was flying. I wanted so much for Jean to share my joy, but he sure wasn't interested in going to a Bible study."

Jean Pronovost considered himself a self-made man. He was proud of his career and the image he projected. He had come a long way from those days in Niagara Falls. At that time, the two top Boston Bruin farm teams were the Flyers, coached by Bill Long, and the Oshawa Generals, coached by Bep Guidlon. Oshawa had Bobby Orr and Wayne Cashman. Niagara Falls had Bernie Parent, Doug

Favell, Derek Sanderson, Gilles Marotte, Don Marcotte, Bill Goldsworthy and Gary Dornhoeffer—all future NHLers.

In those days, Jean had dreamed of playing in the NHL—now he had done it. He earned his living with his skills. He played in a world where egos and a macho image were part of the game. Well respected by his peers, he did not want to risk his reputation by being associated with the Jesus freaks. Why did he need Jesus Christ? He had done alright on his own.

"Probably the two biggest reasons I finally did agree to go to a Bible study were because of the changes in my wife and because of Ed Kea's confidence in life. I remember walking in there like I knew it all, even though I had never read the Bible in my life. I felt pretty uncomfortable hearing them talk about things I had never heard about. It was worse when they prayed. I didn't pray in private, let alone in public. The only time I used the words Jesus Christ was as an expression or as swearing.

"For about three months I really fought it, but it was no use. I realized that the only way I could call myself a Christian was to ask Jesus Christ to save me from my sins. It went against everything I had ever been taught and I was scared, but I didn't want to wait any longer to ask the Lord Jesus Christ to come into my life."

Since then, life has certainly changed for the Pronovosts.

"We have so much more love for each other and the children now," says Jean. "Also, I never used to read the Bible at all, but now I can't get enough. God's Word is a fascinating book."

Diane describes the interest of her parents in understanding what was going on in their lives.

"Through letters and phone calls, they knew something was different and demanded to know what it was. Jean and I shared the gospel with them and they were as amazed as I had been to know they could be assured of life after death and forgiveness from sin. They immediately prayed to receive Jesus Christ. It wasn't long until Jean's parents and other members of both our families became Christians as well. We were so happy, especially for Jean's parents who were in their seventies. It's so exciting to return to Quebec and see how they have grown spiritually."

Jean and Diane were recently in Israel, visiting and acquainting themselves with Bible history and geography. Fighting broke out while they were there, so in case their parents had read the news reports, they decided to phone them to calm their worries. But there was news for Jean as well.

"When Atlanta was shifted to Calgary, I had a feeling I wouldn't be going with them, but didn't know where I would be playing. Diane learned over the phone that we had been traded to the Washington Capitals," says Jean.

After fourteen years of pro hockey, he was not surprised or upset at the move.

"We are really looking forward to our new club and our new home. The Capitals are a young team on the way up. Who knows? Perhaps one of the reasons we were traded is because there is someone there who thinks being a Christian is fanatical and crazy like I used to think," says Jean. "I'll be able to show him there's nothing freaky about it at all. As a matter of fact, it's the most natural thing in life. It is simply being reunited with the God who created us.''

> Then Jesus entered a house, and again a crowd gathered, so that he and his disciples were not even able to eat. When his family heard about this, they went to take charge of him, for they said, ''He is out of his mind.''
>
> Mark 3:20,21

13

Golfer with a Grip on Life
Bill Tape

It was a big day for young Bill Tape. It was his first golf competition, a junior tournament in Maple Downs in Toronto.

A lot had gone into the preparation for that day. At first, he just enjoyed going golfing with his dad in Port Erie, Ontario. But his interest grew, and he soon found himself with his own set of junior clubs. His natural ability, coupled with the help of the club pro at Erie Downs with his fundamentals, exposed the promise of better things to come for the young golf enthusiast. So he spent hours at Erie Downs—practicing, caddying, cleaning clubs, and looking after the electric golf carts.

And now he had a chance to prove himself.

"I really expected big things," remembers Bill. "I wanted to do well because Dad was with me. I wasn't prepared for the pressure that the crowds and other players created. My concentration was terrible and I played worse than I ever had. Consequently, I shot a miserable 95."

The experience left a damaging impression on Bill's hopes for a golf career. During the crucial development years in his late teens, Bill's interests shifted to other sports.

"I played a lot of baseball, and between the ages of seventeen and twenty, I probably played only a half dozen rounds of golf a year," says Bill.

Meanwhile, his hockey talents had attracted attention from Ed Chadwick, a scout for the Pittsburgh Penguins of the NHL.

"They wanted me to report to one of their minor league teams," Bill says. "But after talking to Gary Dornhoeffer, whom I had gotten to know through golf, it didn't take me long to decide that my future as a pro hockey player was not feasible in light of my abilities."

After a brief stint at the University of Buffalo on a hockey scholarship, Bill lost all interest in returning to school. While working in a factory, he decided to accept a position at the Doone Valley Golf Club in Kitchener. That led to his entering the 1968 Canadian Amateur Golf championship to be held at Westmount in Kitchener.

"It was quite an experience," remembers Bill. "I was scared to death, absolutely terrified. I stepped up to the first tee and sent my drive—not only out of bounds, but right out of the golf course and into the backyard swimming pool of one of the houses along the fairway. I teed up another ball and hit it off near the boundary fence. My caddy and I began to casually stroll down the fairway—but we discovered that that ball was out of bounds too.

"So I left my caddy on the fairway, took a 3-wood and a single golf ball and headed back to the tee again. I was really embarrassed and pretty eager to get my game started and away from the gallery. I teed up and hit my third shot out of bounds. One of the guys playing behind me threw me a ball as he was getting impatient. I teed that one up and hit it out of bounds! Finally, I got my fifth ball in play. The hole was a par 5, and I made a 13.

"In spite of the opening disaster, I wound up with a respectable 81. I was also the hit of the press with my first-hole antics, and got more coverage than the day's leading golfer."

It wasn't long until Bill turned professional, working out of Westmount. Playing in the Canadian Open at the Richilieu Valley Courses in Montreal led to a conversation with Gary Player which opened up a whole new vista of golf experience for Bill. His international career was about to begin.

"I decided to go on the South American tour and had my eyes opened by the quality of golf I saw there. Eventually I played in Japan, the Spanish Open, the Madrid Open and the Portuguese Open. But I had yet to win a major tournament. On previous occasions, I had come close but faltered in the last round," says Bill. "I came closest while playing in the French Open in 1974.

"At the end of the first nine holes of the final day's round, I was tied for the lead at three under par. I could taste victory when the pressure overcame me. I had three bogeys on the last nine holes and ended up in fourth place overall.

"The pressures of the pro tour just grind away at you. All the emotions you experience in life may be forced upon you on the golf course in one round of golf—fear, joy, sadness, doubt, worry and excitement all combine to create tremendous pressure. I could never control the pressure because I never firmly believed in my mechanics. I had always mistrusted my ability, and as a result, was constantly changing my swing or grip to improve. Fear was my main enemy, and my muscles responded to the way I felt. It took me a long time to realize you just don't hit it perfect all the time. Nobody does," remembers Bill.

The following winter found Bill in Florida, living with other aspiring golfers and working on his game. It was there he met Tommy Thomas, a golf pro from Ohio, who shared condominium expenses with Bill and the others.

"I had done a lot of travelling, and I still had not found meaning and fulfillment in life," says Bill. "I had tried it all, but had no satisfaction or answers. Tommy really amazed me. He would tell me all these wild and fascinating things that the Bible had to say about the end of the world and the return of the Lord Jesus Christ. I had attended Sunday School for a while as a kid, but most of my Sundays were spent on the golf course as a caddy. I had never heard of all this stuff, and I really wanted to know if it was truth or just a lot of malarkey.

"I returned home to Fort Erie for Christmas and looked up an old friend for some answers. I had always considered him religious and I knew I could trust him to answer all the questions I had. It turned out that he had become a Christian and had been praying for my conversion for six months. We stayed up until all hours of the morning talking, until finally I, too, asked the Lord Jesus to be my Savior and forgive my sins. I felt like a terrible load had been lifted off my shoulders. I felt new and fresh and clean and so thankful. I just wanted to tell everybody, and could hardly believe that others didn't seem to want what I had just found.

"My family figured I was off on another tangent,

that I had totally flipped out and lost my marbles," remembers Bill.

Always an extremely emotional person, Bill rejoiced in his new feelings. He headed back to Florida—and trouble.

Just as he had allowed his feelings to determine his behavior on the golf course, he began to let his feelings control his new Christian life. One of the most difficult things Christians have to learn is that behavior is to be controlled by our thinking, not by feelings. Our thinking is guided by the written, indestructible Word of God—the Bible. Feelings fluctuate; the Word of God is the same yesterday, today and forever.

"I had no contact with other Christians, and when the feelings wore off, I soon began to doubt all that had happened," says Bill. "As much as I hated it, I began to drift back into my old way of life. I had a gospel tape in my car that I used to hide and play when I was alone.

"I returned to Canada and played out of Toronto's National Club. With a lot of hard work and a lot of help from Al Balding, I won the 1975 Canadian Professional Golf Association Championship and was invited to represent Canada in the World Cup in Bangkok, Thailand. It was the peak of my career."

Bill had won the Manitoba Open in 1974, but it couldn't compare with this feat. He was now the top pro golfer in Canada. It was a dramatic win—sinking a three-foot putt on the final hole and edging out George Knudson by one shot. His prize money was $10,000 and expense paid invitations were offered to tournaments all over the world. He was the center of media attention with cameras and microphones ready to catch his every word and expression.

"It was a dream come true," says Bill. "After all those years I was on top of the world. Yet only one month later, the money and the people were gone. I sadly realized that even this wasn't lasting. It was one of many other honors and goals that I had strived for only to find them an illusion. I then realized that meeting Jesus Christ was the greatest thing that had ever happened to me—He would last forever. Now I can't imagine ever trying to live in this world without the Lord Jesus Christ."

Because of his celebrity status, Bill was asked to speak at a minor hockey banquet in Toronto, where he met two other speakers and brothers in Christ, Peter Muller and Zenon Andrusyshyn of the Argos. He was uplifted by their fellowship and they invited him to an Athletes In Action conference in Winnipeg.

"I was very aware of my need for fellowship and encouragement, and I left the banquet very thankful to the Lord for introducing me to Peter and Zee," says Bill. "I really looked forward to going to the conference after returning from Thailand."

The World Cup was a disaster and proved to be a humbling and embarrassing experience for Bill. Physical sickness and poor play combined to defeat him. Returning home, he looked forward to the Winnipeg conference.

While waiting at the airport to leave for Winnipeg, he met Mel Stevens of Teen Ranch, also headed for the AIA conference. It was the beginning of a relationship that grew and lasted over the years.

Greatly strengthened by the AIA conference and being able to share his faith openly with other athletes, Bill returned home in good spirits. Through

Mel, he contacted another Christian athlete, Ron Ellis. Ellis had just returned from the Toronto Maple Leafs and was managing the Carrying Place Country Club in Toronto. He was looking for a head golf pro. Bill was soon hired to fill the vacancy.

Then in October of 1976, God brought another important person into Bill's life. He was asked to be an escort at the Oktoberfest celebrations in Kitchener. A past queen of the pageant, a former Miss California, was also in attendance as co-host.

"I had been looking and looking and searching for the right woman for me," says Bill. "When I least expected it, the Lord introduced me to Gayle Gorrell. Bingo!—it was love at first sight for both of us. Six months later, we were married in California."

The Tapes now reside in California. Bill gave up playing tournament golf just prior to his son Jeffrey's birth in 1978. The man who used to work on his golf grip, is now working on another kind of grip.

"We pray at the table and sixteen-month-old Jeffrey holds hands with Gayle and me," says Bill. "Usually, as soon as the prayer is finished, Jeffrey will say, 'AMEN!' "

Let us hold unswervingly to the hope we profess, for he who promised is faithful.
Hebrews 10:23

14

Two Big Decisions
Michel Dion

Michel Dion has faced two major decisions in his life. The first one concerned his professional athletic career. The second one, his life.

At the age of 17 years, Michel was already a highly prized commodity. He had been a member of the Montreal Junior Canadiens for two years. At the tender age of 15, he was one of two goalies on a Memorial Cup championship team. Coached by Roger Bedard, the Junior Canadiens (with the likes of Gilbert Perrault, Richard Martin, Bobby Lalonde and Jocelyn Gouvremont), captured Canada's prized junior hockey championship.

But Michel had not seen too much ice time in his first two years. He was young, and it takes years to develop as a goal-tender. In fact, the Canadiens felt he should be patient and satisfied that he was a part of the team at all. The Canadien organization was like a big family—indeed, the royal family of hockey. But Michel felt differently.

"I wanted to play pro hockey and I couldn't understand how I was going to improve by sitting on the bench," says Michel. "I had sacrificed a lot to play hockey and I didn't feel I was appreciated."

So when the Montreal Expos of the National Baseball League came bearing gifts, they found a receptive young man. Besides being a goalie, Michel was an outstanding young baseball product of the Montreal junior leagues. Rather than catching pucks, he would be catching baseballs and calling the signals behind the plate. It would be a real publicity coup for the Expos to sign a hometown player—so they offered to sign Michel as a free agent, with one major stipulation. He had to quit playing hockey. They were not going to risk their investment in Michel by having him stopping pucks in the winter time.

Goalies are a strange breed. They go against the natural human reaction of getting out of the way of an object that is directed towards them. Men duck bullets and punches. But a goal-tender earns his living by putting his body or any part of it in the path of a puck travelling up to 100 m.p.h.

"I was trapped between two loves," remembers Michel. "I loved both sports. But I felt that my chances of succeeding were greater in baseball than hockey. I signed with the Expos in September of 1971. This meant that I couldn't play for the Junior Canadiens that winter since I would be reporting to spring training with the Expos Class A farm team in Palm Beach, Florida.

"It was a difficult winter for me. I would go to the Jr. Canadiens' games and feel like an outsider. The team treated me like I had betrayed them and most of my teammates were disappointed in me."

Winter soon passed, however, and Michel made his way south to prepare for his new career. But he soon realized that playing in Palm Beach on one of many Expo farm teams could not compare with playing for

151

the number one development team of the Montreal Canadiens. As much as he enjoyed playing baseball, he was not overly enthusiastic with the baseball way of life in the minors. The clincher came when he found out that the parent Expos had recently signed another junior hockey player, but did not force him to give up his hockey career.

"After the season was over, I returned to Montreal and asked the Expos to let me continue with my hockey career as well," states Michel. "Then I swallowed my pride and asked the Junior Canadiens if I could return. They had me play both Junior "B" and Junior "A" to compensate for my year off. I was being reminded that I wasn't one of their favorite players because of what I had done."

For the next two years, Michel completed his junior career with the Canadiens and gave up on the Expos' baseball offer. They were two difficult years. His play was not outstanding and he was a very confused young man. His great love was sports, and by making an unwise decision, he had almost lost both his professional careers. But how long would he have to go on paying for his mistake?

He developed a bad attitude—which resulted in less ice time and which further frustrated Michel and the Montreal organization. He couldn't wait for his junior career to end when he would be eligible for the NHL draft.

"I was shocked when I wasn't drafted by the NHL and was selected only in the seventh round of the World Hockey Association draft," says Michel. "The Indianapolis Racers, who drafted me, already had enough goalies, so they sent me to the minors. I got a lot of ice time while playing for Mohawk Valley in the North American League, but my baseball days came back to haunt me. An old knee injury, suffered while sliding into second base, flared up and I had to have my cartilage removed.''

It wasn't until the following year, after being sent to the minors again, that coach Brian Conacher called Michel in and told him that Racer goalie Andy Brown was hurt. This was his chance to stay with the big club. He did stay—and ended the season with the best goals against average in the WHA, winning the Ben Hatskin trophy.

Michel was the Racers' number one goalie the next year until the club changed owners and Nelson Skalbania entered the Indianapolis sporting scene. Although the Racers played in the brand new and beautiful Market Square Arena, they were having trouble drawing fans. Indiana is the home of basketball and college football. Hoosier fans are more familiar with Purdue and Indiana rivalries with Ohio State than with hockey. Even high school basketball and football games sometimes outdrew the Racers. In the annual Kentucky-Indiana All-Star high school basketball game, close to 17,000 fans crowded into Market Square Arena.

Skalbania ordered salary cuts and brought in his own people to try and create a winner and a crowd-pleaser. The new coach, Ron Ingram, favored goalie Gary Inness. Michel followed coach Jacques Demers 90 miles down Interstate 74 to the Cincinnati Coliseum, home of the Cincinnati Stingers.

Michel had that old feeling of not being appreciated again and said goodbye to Indianapolis. But there was one person who appreciated him.

As a bachelor attempting to cook his own meals, he cut himself with a kitchen knife and the wound became badly infected. When he visited an emergency ward, he met his future wife, Karla.

After two years in Cincinnati, the WHA was absorbed by the NHL, and Michel found himself back in his home province playing for the Quebec Nordiques. He was their number one man in the nets, sharing the goaltending workload with Ron Lowe and Goren Hogostra. Michel had finally made the NHL and did so in style. Interestingly enough, he outperformed, in the long run, the goalies who years earlier had forced him to sit on the bench with the Junior Canadiens. Michel proved to be durable, a survivor.

By this time, Michel had made another major decision—one that would save his life. With all his travelling in pro hockey, it was difficult to attend church and Michel had long ago lost interest in anything religious.

"It had been quite a few years since I had really thought about religion," says Michel. "When two teammates in Cincinnati, Dave Forbes and Chuck Luksa, invited me to a pre-game chapel, I was interested in attending. I had heard about a lot of beliefs and cults, but after attending a few times, I realized that if you are looking for truth, you might as well go to the source—the Bible.

"We were on the road a couple of weeks later in Quebec City when, after leaving chapel, Chuck stunned and offended me. He asked me if I was a Christian and I said I was."

Michel's reaction to this crucial question was revealing. Even though he had given up on his religious background, at this moment of decision he immediately reached out for support to something that for years he had considered weak.

"Chuck responded by showing me from the Bible that what I had always thought a Christian was, did not coincide with what the Bible said. As offended as I was, I asked some more questions and demanded that Chuck give me answers. My spiritual life was of more importance than my hockey career, and long ago I had almost lost that because of an unwise decision. I wasn't going to make the same mistake twice. I soon realized that what Chuck was saying and what the chapel speaker, Don Liesemer, had said made a lot of sense. I then made the wisest and greatest decision I have ever made—I asked the Lord Jesus Christ to be my Savior."

Later, Michel made an off-season trip to Phoenix where he met other professional Christian athletes. It opened up a whole new world of awareness for him.

"I try to encourage other players to ask questions and keep searching," says Michel. "We all have the same needs that can only be met by the Lord Jesus Christ. A lot of them are probably just as scared as I once was and refuse to ask questions as I once did. But if they will only keep searching, they will find the Truth."

Michel Dion is in a good position to help someone when he is faced with a decision. He knows from experience what it is to make the wrong one—and the right one.

Jesus answered, "I am the way and the truth and the life. No one comes to the Father except through me."   John 14:6

15

When the Fun Ran Out
Peter Muller

Peter Muller realized that he was going to have to make some changes in his life. He was a scholarship athlete at the University of Western Illinois, but he was just one of many other scholarship athletes on campus. Playing football for Lawrence Park Collegiate in Toronto, he had been one of the better players on the team. Now, playing for the University of Western Illinois Leathernecks, he was amongst players who **all** had outstanding careers at their respective high schools.

"There were some major differences I noticed right away," remembers Peter. "I had been close to my high school coaches Jack Green, Ed Saunders and Gene Nesterenko. Now, I was just one of many players trying to please ex-Alouette coach Darrell Mudra. All our moves on the field would be filmed and we came under close examination. We weren't just watched; we were analyzed. That sure was different from the days at Lawrence Park, when one of the teachers used to film our games from the school roof as a hobby. We'd all get together afterward and have a hotdog session, watching ourselves perform on the field."

Muller had entered into a new level of competition and tension, and performance requirements were elevated. The weekend that he and his dad had visited the campus where he was to spend the next four years of his life was a distant memory. Since Peter had come highly recommended, the school and coaches had rolled out the red carpet to welcome the Mullers and make them feel at home. But now it was time to produce.

"As a freshman, I lost the starting quarterback job to Steve. He was really competitive and I considered him a real jerk," recalls Peter. "He didn't go along with the rest of us. He was just different."

Peter felt a real need to belong, to be accepted by his teammates. Being a Canadian on a U.S. campus was difficult enough, without adding any other reasons for rejection.

"I was thrilled just to be a part of the whole scene, and what my teammates thought of me was very important. I joined a fraternity and was exposed to a lot of different values and lifestyles. I was never into drinking in high school, but here it was different; everybody did it," recalls Peter.

Everybody except Steve Mikez.

There is a Walt's Bar in every college town. It is the "in" place. Cheap beer and good times are had by all. Athletes gather round and swap stories, and others gather round to listen. Peter spent a lot of time in Walt's Bar; he was one of the boys; he was accepted.

"Quarterbacks are moody to begin with, so my relationship to Steve did not really improve until I was switched to wide receiver and tight end with the Varsity in my second and third years," says

Peter.

Some people grow up and spread good cheer; Peter grew up and just spread. As a freshman he was 6'1'' and 190 lbs. By the time he was graduated, he was 6'4½'' and 230 lbs.

"By our third year," Peter recalls, "Steve had been red-shirted [kept out for a year to extend his eligibility], so there was really no competition between us anymore. I began taking a longer look at him.

"There were many nights I'd close Walt's Bar and wobble and weave the fifteen-minute walk home. In a way, I enjoyed those walks—they gave me a chance to be alone. The streets were quiet and I'd do a lot of thinking. I was really getting tired of my lifestyle. It was a lot of fun, but the fun had run out. Deep down I knew that this wasn't where it was at," remembers Peter.

"I began to talk to Steve. He seemed to have it all together. I'd make sure we were alone so no one would see us. If someone saw us together, I'd just joke about it since Steve was still the jerk; he was too straight. He would talk about the Bible with me and I'd try to shoot him down. But deep inside I was hoping he would destroy my arguments and questions. I wanted to believe as he did."

One day Steve read through a pamphlet called the Four Spiritual Laws with Peter. Even though at the time he didn't fully understand the scope and consequences of what he did, Peter prayed with Steve to receive the Lord Jesus Christ.

"For months I was torn between my old friends and my new faith," says Peter. "I was really afraid to be identified with Steve and his friends as I still wanted to be accepted by the others. I didn't want to be considered a jerk. I made some real efforts at giving my old lifestyle another crack, but as I read the Bible more and hung around with other Christians, I soon realized the uselessness of my previous existence.

"Take a simple thing like the name Jesus Christ—I had never used it except in a swearing context. Now I found myself reacting inside when others did the same. It really bothered me. I wasn't used to praying either. I was a successful athlete who could overcome any obstacle. It took me a while to realize that I could now go to a greater Person than I could ever hope to be."

The incident that shook Peter off the fence occurred in his senior year. The Athletes In Action wrestling team was coming to campus and Peter was asked to look after them.

"As I watched them and listened to them, I realized that they were impressive athletes. I was really strengthened by the fact you could be a Christian **and** an outstanding athlete."

The guy who was afraid of ridicule, afraid of being called a jerk, afraid of being publicly associated with Christians, took his stand.

"I felt a little uncomfortable as I sat on the bench with the AIA wrestlers. After all, I was a Leatherneck and here I was sitting with a visiting team in front of 3,000 die-hard Leatherneck fans. It felt good though, for I was saying, 'I'm one of them; I believe in the same thing they believe in; they believe in the same thing I believe in.'

"From that point on," Peter recalls, "I really started to grow spiritually."

Peter's athletic career took off as well. Turning down offers from Washington and New England of the NFL to be their punter, he returned to Toronto to try out with the Argos as a tight end.

"I felt a little uneasy the first time in the huddle," recalls Peter. "Here I was standing beside Bill Symons, a guy I used to idolize as a kid watching the Argo games. I wasn't sure I was supposed to be there."

The Argos thought differently, and Peter has had a long and productive career in the CFL. He has been nominated for the coveted Schenley Award three times in his eight-year career. He has been the recipient of both the Tom Pate Memorial Award and the Shopsy Most Valuable Player Award. Peter ranks fourth on the all-time Argo pass reception list and was voted Mississauga's Professional Athlete of the Year in 1978.

"One of my most exciting games was when quarterback Mike Rae and I combined to score the fastest three touchdowns in one game against the Alouettes. Although it took him a little longer to do it, Johnny Rogers scored three for Montreal, and we ended up losing the game," says Peter.

Other memories are not as pleasant.

"The most shocking period of my life was when I travelled in the spring of 1978. I started out in Europe with stops in Africa, Bombay, Indonesia, Malaysia, Bangkok and Hong Kong. I was very interested in missionary work, and I visited workers on the mission fields. Coming from our comfortable North American society, I found it hard to believe the poverty, suffering, disease and unsanitary living conditions in parts of our world.

"I also spent some time at the Dalat School for the

children of missionaries. Their parents work in all parts of Asia, and these kids are all flown in and separated from their parents while being centrally educated.

"I support missionary work and would like to be involved in it at some point in my life. But my primary responsibility right now is to my family, to be a better son and brother. Also, at present I feel a strong responsibility to my fellow athletes.

"I get discouraged at times with people's images of Christianity. I've talked to teammates who think I'm involved in a cult; who think they will be shoved into a box and stereotyped. If I could only make them understand that I truly love them as people and want to share my joy with them. If they would only see that Christianity is not just obeying commandments, but also the only true vehicle toward a free and liberating life."

Peter is proud to be an Argo despite the comments of those who treat the CFL club as a national joke. It has been 28 years since the Argos have won the Grey Cup, and there are few who have been with the Argos longer and felt the frustration as much.

Yet Peter is human. No athlete wants to spend the off-season in a cast or injured. After months of emotional and physical punishment, he looks forward to being able to relax and renew himself. Thus, athletes tend to hold back in meaningless games—games with nothing at stake—for fear of injury. The Argos, knocked out of the play-offs, were involved in such a season-ending game with the Ottawa Rough Riders.

"It was late in the second quarter, and the lights came on. My mind flashed back to the times when I would go down to the CNE and watch the Argos

161

play. I'd sit way up in section T and watch in awe. It was all so mystical and beautiful under the lights. Suddenly I realized how selfish I was, not putting out to the best of my ability. How many others would just love to be in my position? Here I was, my dream had come true, and I didn't appreciate it. I wasn't being fair to my coaches and teammates, the fans, even the other team, as they were professionals and expected me to play like a professional. I wasn't being fair to God who gave me all the talent that I was wasting. I felt ashamed and foolish—and for the rest of the game, I turned it on.

"I had played almost half a game before I realized how foolish I was. Thankfully, I still had time left to correct the situation.

"I learned a valuable lesson from that experience. I look around and see others at various stages of the game of life. I urge them to realize that it's not too late—there is still time left on the clock—to correct their relationship to Jesus Christ. It's a terrible feeling to sit at the end of a game and wish you would have played better or put out more effort. But the game is over; it's too late to change it. Who can describe the despair that one would feel if he reached the end of his life, came face to face with Jesus Christ and realized how foolish he was to have rejected Him? But then it would be too late; the game of life would have ended!"

Peter Muller's game plan for the rest of his life is simply this: he will tell anyone who will listen about a Person he once was ashamed of but whom he now worships—Jesus Christ.

Therefore I tell you that no one who is

speaking by the Spirit of God says, 'Jesus be cursed,' and no one can say, 'Jesus is Lord,' except by the Holy Spirit.   I Corinthians 12:3

16

The World at His Fingertips
Ron Ellis

Jan Greenlaw rushed to her seat in the Kitchener Auditorium. She had hurried over from Toronto and had arrived in time to see the Toronto Maple Leafs and the New York Rangers in their pre-game warm-up. Both teams were using these exhibition games to prepare for the upcoming 1964-65 NHL season.

Jan was so excited; the man who was to be her future husband was wearing a Maple Leaf jersey. She had known him since grade four, when they were both nine years old. He had sacrificed and worked hard as a Junior "A" player with the Toronto Marlboros, preparing for his professional career. During that time, they had to be satisfied with getting together after the Friday night home games. He used to hit the books for two hours every night since he considered his schooling very important. With all the practices and games, very little time was left for the couple to be together.

But it had all been worth it. There he was skating around, firing pucks at the goalies with all the other NHL stars she had watched many times on television. Seated behind the goal, she banged the glass and jumped up and down to let him know she was there watching.

One very proud rookie, with axe handle shoulders and brush cut, noticed Jan jumping up and down. Ron Ellis turned away quickly and pretended not to notice her. He was embarrassed. Ron laughs now, but remembers, "I was really shy then. I talked to Janny after the game and told her that just wasn't the way it was done."

Ronnie had cracked the star-studded Leaf line-up. The team had just won three Stanley cups in a row. Although Ron still had a year of Junior eligibility left, coach Punch Imlach felt he would benefit more by being with the Leafs.

Ellis was a prized possession. Most teams sent a scout to check out a 15-year-old prospect with potential. But when the Leafs went courting, they put their best foot forward. Punch Imlach and King Clancy came to visit the Ellis family when they lived in Ottawa. They discussed the idea of Ron coming to Toronto to play for their top farm team, the Toronto Marlboros hockey club.

Ron's father encouraged his son to accept the Toronto offer, believing Ron had the ability to play for the Leafs and that it was in his best interests to do so.

"It was quite a step for me," recalls Ron. "I had never really been away from home before, but at this stage in my life I began to realize that if I worked hard, it would be possible for me to play professional hockey."

The life of a junior hockey player is one of sacrifice and pressure. Ron had to give up the other sports he enjoyed playing to devote full time to hockey skills development. He was an excellent student despite the heavy practice and travel schedule. His every move was watched by scouts as they charted the progress of the young men who they hoped would someday make the big club. "I had always wanted to play for the Leafs, so it was a real treat as a junior to play our home games in Maple Leaf Gardens. We used to draw 8-9,000 people per game."

Ron's final year of junior hockey was as a member of a powerhouse. The Marlies were loaded with talent and the roster was filled with men who would spend long and successful careers in the NHL. Ellis was the team's top goal scorer. The club destroyed its opponents and won the Memorial Cup, symbolizing Canadian junior hockey supremacy. Ron shared Most Valuable Player honors with teammate Peter Stemkowski and finished right behind future Montreal speedster and star Yvan Cournoyer in the All-Star selection for right wingers.

A major decision had to be made by the young Ellis. Ned Harkness of Cornell University in Ithaca, N.Y., was in the midst of building an NCAA hockey dynasty. The Ivy Leaguers had already recruited a young unknown goalie by the name of Ken Dryden. Ned wanted the best; he wanted good hockey players with good grades. He wanted Ronnie Ellis. Punch Imlach had a team loaded with veterans; he wanted to groom the best of the rookie crop to replace them. He wanted Ronnie Ellis to turn professional with the Leafs.

"Looking back," remembers Ron, "I think the main reason I chose to turn pro was that it seemed to be a short-cut to success. The university route would have taken four years. But by turning pro I would be making big money immediately. Janny and I were planning on getting married and the pro career seemed to offer the best opportunity. Therefore, I chose to turn pro and continue my schooling part-time at York University.''

Imlach didn't promise anything, but the hard-working rookie soon found himself on a line with superstars Andy Bathgate and Frank Mahovlich. In his first home game, he scored his first NHL goal against Eddie Johnston of the Boston Bruins.

"My first year as a Leaf was an exciting one. It was a dream come true. I had worked hard for many years, and I was playing with some great pros like Bobby Pulford, Davey Keon and Tim Horton—guys I had followed for years.''

Finishing behind Rookie Award winner Roger Crozier of the Detroit Red Wings, Ellis went on to score 23 goals in a pre-expansion league that considered 20 an excellent season. Indeed, he tied Frank Mahovlich for most goals. Though briefly benched because of a knee injury, Ron enjoyed fourteen productive seasons with the Leafs, including a Stanley Cup winner in 1967. His familiar two-way play, up and down the boards, was a trademark in Maple Leaf Gardens for years.

Ron and Jan were married after his second season. They did not encounter the problems so many young couples do. They had a new car, brand new furniture in a brand new huge apartment, lovely honeymoon, and all the material luxuries and conveniences that a successful young couple could desire.

A major highlight of his career was the role he played in the unforgettable Team Canada versus Russia Series of 1972. Early in training camp, he was put on a line with fellow Leaf Paul Henderson and Bobby Clarke of the Philadelphia Flyers. They were one of the more successful units and the only line to stay intact during the series.

"I was fortunate that I was there to enjoy the greatest experience that a pro hockey player could ever be involved in," recalls Ron. "My linemates and I were good solid two-way hockey players. Team Canada coaches and management probably felt we would get in one or two games, but somehow we jelled in training camp."

Oh, how they jelled! They played in all eight games, with Henderson scoring the winning goals in the last three.

"It was an experience I'll never forget," continued Ellis, "and I'm sure Paul and I will be talking about it for many years to come. We went through so much as a team and had such an impact on Canada. We just couldn't believe the tens of thousands of people at the airports in Montreal and Toronto."

Ronnie Ellis was at the top of his profession. He was idolized by thousands. He had married his grade school sweetheart. Money was never a problem. Anyone who looked at him would wince with envy and wish they were in his shoes. Ronnie Ellis had the world at his fingertips—or did he?

"I was having problems coping with the realities of life, the pressures of my career. Scoring goals and winning games became the most important objective in my life. I'd score a hat trick one night, and immediately begin worrying about how long it would be until my next goal. If you went a few games without scoring, or the team went five or six games without a win, you were in the pressure cooker.

"The Stanley Cup is a goal every pro hockey player strives for. Some players are in the league for years and never get to play on a winner, yet the Leafs won in my third year. That thrill did not last. Memories and celebrations fade away. I began to wonder where this happiness was that I was striving for. I thought it would come by being an NHL star, financially sound, or a Stanley Cup winner.

"I had no purpose in life other than chasing a black puck around the ice. Was that all I was to contribute to the world, to humanity? Everything that I had worked and strived for—what would happen to it when I died? What would happen to me when I died?

"Very few people realized that I was in turmoil. I would put on a mask, a happy mask to let everyone think that life was great. Jan knew though. She knew how insecure and selfish I was. She knew how moody and gloomy I could be. I was very unhappy with the type of person I had become. Ronnie Ellis played against the toughest men in the NHL, but it was Janny Ellis who was strongest at this point in our lives."

One day during this time of searching and painful growth. Ron entered the dressing room after practice to find that some very unusual gifts had been placed in the player's cubicles. Each player had been given a beautiful blue Bible with the Maple Leaf crest and his name on the front.

"I was fairly quiet; I didn't really know how to react," recalls Ron. "I felt it would be a very nice addition to our home. If someone saw it, it wouldn't be too embarrassing as it had the Leaf crest and I could always say it was sort of a souvenir of my Leaf days.

"Paul and Eleanor Henderson would spend a lot of time with Jan and I, and Paul and I were close on the endless road trips. Our discussions would usually revolve around the concepts of life and religion, and the existence of God. Paul finally overcame my stubbornness and talked me into going out to meet the man who had given us the Bibles.''

The upshot was that Jan and Ron decided to attend an athlete's retreat at Teen Ranch in Caledon, north of Toronto. They really did not know what to expect. Greeted by Mel Stevens and his wife, Janet, Ron and Jan felt immediately at home.

Teen Ranch is a year-round Christian camp founded in 1972. Many of the campers at the camp, including Greg Millen, John Anderson, and Doug Jarvis, have gone on to professional careers of their own. A large full-time staff supervises activities including English and Western riding, outdoor education, week-end camps and hockey school. Mel also leads chapel services and Bible studies for the Leafs and Argos and the ranch has become a popular retreat for athletes and their families.

''The people we met gave us the feeling we had known them for a long time,'' remembers Ron. ''It was something new and strange for Janny and I. In the world of pro sports, you meet a lot of people, but you will probably never see them again and you usually forget them immediately. We really enjoyed ourselves, and it suddenly dawned on me there was no booze, no dirty jokes—just a group of athletes and their families enjoying the outdoors and each other's company. We would have discussions and I would just listen to these fellow pros discuss the Bible or God. They seemed to have their lives in perspective; they were so confident and content. I was very interested because I certainly did not have peace of mind and I did not have the purpose in life these people had—to glorify the Lord.

''Jan and I left with a lot to think about. I had to go up north to our cottage for a few days and it enabled us both to be alone. I came to the conclusion that I wanted to have this personal relationship with God. I wanted to have that peace, purpose and joy that the other athletes and their families had. I decided then and there to ask Jesus Christ to forgive my sin and be Lord of my life.

"Upon returning home, I walked into the house and Janny was all excited. She told me she had asked Jesus Christ into her life while I was gone. Then I shared some of my own excitement with her."

Ron retired from the Leafs at the end of training camp in 1975. He spent two years operating a Sporting Complex which included a golf course. He surprised the hockey world when he resigned, and he surprised it again when he decided to come back. In 1977, Canada entered the World Cup Hockey Championships in Vienna, Austria. With no assurance of a spot on the team, but knowing he wanted to return, the disciplined and dedicated athlete planned his comeback.

"For five months I drove up to Bradford and was on the ice at seven in the morning. I skated and forced myself to do stops and starts. I would shoot at a goalie who agreed to come out with me. It was tough and many times I wondered if I could do it. Two years is a long time off skates."

Despite his doubts, Ron was again selected to play for Team Canada in international competition. Now a bigger decision had to be made: should he return to the NHL?

After he returned to the Leafs, Ron remembers how grateful he was to meet other pro athletes who had Jesus Christ in their lives: "I had always blamed the game for my problems and depression and my lack of enjoyment in life. I now realized that I had been given many talents and I wanted to use them to glorify the Lord Jesus Christ and share with my teammates what He had done in my life.''

Life and times have changed for Jan and Ronnie and their two children, Kitty ....d R.J. (Ron Jr.). Life's problems continue, but now they can draw on a living power to deal with and overcome them.

Ron's career continues with the Leafs—he now has over 1,000 games and 330 goals under his belt. But his priorities have changed. "Our family life has become very happy and very close. We want to make our friends and families aware that we love them dearly, Also, the chapel program has begun in the NHL and has been well received. A lot of the younger players in the League will be exposed early in their careers to the good news of Christ.''

Many players will be attracted to the gospel because it is being spread by Ronnie Ellis, the successful and respected NHL veteran. As they encounter frustrations and disappointments in their pro careers, as the aura of success and achievement dims, as they begin to search for meaning in their lives, they will have someone to turn to. Ron Ellis will gladly try to end their dissatisfaction by sharing with them the secret that changed his life—a relationship with Jesus Christ.

Follow my example, as I follow the example of Christ.   **I Corinthians 11:1**

Letter From the Author
To Tommy...From Coach

Dear Tommy,

As the goalie on the hockey team I coached, you were always Number One in the program. When asked to write this book, I wanted to make it personal, so I wrote it to you—and through you, to every athlete, coach, fan and sportswriter, no matter what their sport.

The athletes you read about are just like you and me; they all had childhood dreams, played at all different levels. They've trained, and hurt and cried. They have had to swallow their pride in failure, and have soared in success. They have all done the wild and crazy things which usually accompany being a part of any team.

These are people who have set goals and attained them. But they grew dissatisfied with their achievements and rewards; all these failed to measure up to their expectations. They hit the top and asked, **"Is that all there is?"**

Tommy, these athletes reached the peak of their

abilities through skill—but also due to the desire and confidence they had in themselves. During their careers they received fame and adulation; their self-images and egos grew even bigger.

Yet, in a quiet moment, they came to their Creator as creatures. They admitted there was One greater than themselves. They admitted there was something they could not do. They reached out their hands in faith to the only Person who could make right their relationship with God—Jesus Christ. At that moment, Tommy, they added another dimension to their lives—they became children of God.

Every athlete wants to get the most money and the best contract he can for his skills. He yearns to play for the highest bidder. The athletes in this book received a contract no owner can match. NO-CUT, NO-TRADE—FOREVER! They are FREE AGENTS!

You don't have to leave your mind in your equipment bag to become a Christian. You don't have to have blind faith or "faith in faith." You don't have to put your helmet on backwards, close your eyes, hold your nose and leap into the dark.

Historic Christianity has honest answers to honest questions. No one knows everything—but you don't have to be satisfied with "just believe." Base your faith on the work of Jesus Christ on the cross. Historically, theologically, experientially—it happened.

If you had been on your way home from practice and passed by the cross, you would have seen his dislocated shoulders and spastic hands as spikes cut the nerves. You would have heard the screaming, the moans, the grunts and the laughter. You would have smelled the waste and stench. Your mouth would have been dry from the dust and the awful sight before you. You could have touched his body with your trembling hands.

As athletes, Tommy, we must all face the day when injuries overwhelm, when legs tire, when rookies as hungry as we once were take our jobs away from us. Wise is the man who plans for the future. As humans, we cannot escape the fact that we will physically die. No matter how hard we try to escape reality, evading this thought by losing ourselves in various forms of distraction and entertainment, we must all face that quiet moment of silence when we realize that day will come.

Plan, Tommy. Invest. For just as certain as your athletic career will soon end and you must prepare for the next stage of your life, your physical life is going to end as well. What plans or investments have you made for where you will spend eternity? Scripture leaves only two options: eternal life or eternal death.

There are no tie games in this league. You either win or you lose. You are either for Christ or you are against Him.

But you will never make this team by your own efforts. As an athlete, constantly having to have yourself rated and having to better yourself, you must nevertheless accept that you can never become worthy of being accepted by Christ—no matter how hard you train and sweat, no matter how good you are.

Tommy, if your two biggest goals in life were to play for the Toronto Maple Leafs and become a Christian, these are some ways you could achieve them: You could go to a sports store and buy a Leaf jersey or you could go to a jewelry store and buy a cross—neither would work. You could go to Maple

Leaf Gardens or go to a church—neither would work. You could pay extra money to a scalper or put extra money in the collection plate—neither would work. You could read the sports pages and learn all about the team, or you could read the Bible and learn all about God—neither would work. You could carry around a baby picture of yourself wearing a Leaf hat and tell everybody you play for the Leafs and show them your picture as proof, or you could be baptized and confirmed telling everyone you are a Christian—but neither would work. You could go to the Royal York Hotel and eat with the players at their pre-game meal or you could take communion— neither would be enough. You could ask someone to put in a good word with the owner and he'll say it depends on what the coach thinks, or you can rely on a minister or priest and God will say it depends on **your** relationship to Christ.

It's foolish to think of becoming a Leaf in the ways we've mentioned, isn't it? It is just as foolish to think of becoming a Christian by these means. The way to earn a spot on the Toronto Maple Leafs is to work hard on your fundamentals, play college or junior hockey, go to training camp and excel in the exhibition games. If your skill level and desire are acceptable, they will sign you.

The way to become a Christian is to believe that Jesus Christ came to save all people and to ask Him to save you. You could boast about making the Leafs; you could say with pride, "I did it." You can't boast about becoming a Christian. You can say with joy, "Christ did it for me."

I loved you when you played for me. But I look back on it now and realize it was both a selfish and an idealistic love. You worked so hard that I loved you—

and because you worked even harder, I loved you more. My love for you was based on what you did or did not do, rather than on who you were.

I love you now Tommy as I have never loved you before. You could let in three goals from outside the blueline in the first period of the final game and it would not affect this love. This love is based on truth, on reality. It is unshakeable. As a creature of God, I love you as a fellow creature. As a sinner who has found God, I love you as a sinner who's still searching for God. I am no better than you. I am as unworthy as you of being saved by Jesus Christ. I deserve God's grace no more than you do—a grace that gives us what we don't deserve. God's mercy protects us from what we do deserve.

May God continue to draw you to Him and, if it be His will, to further your athletic career. I pray for the day when students will be in a high school auditorium and the guest speaker will rise and say, "Hi, my name is Tommy. I'm a Christian."

Go for it, Tommy. Take it to the limit!

Sincerely,

Coach Talentino

The Four Spiritual Laws

You probably bought and read this book because of the people in it. They are all successful and exceptional athletes. But the reason they agreed to appear in this book and share their lives with you is to point you to Another, the Lord Jesus Christ. If you sense your need of Jesus Christ, you are not alone; there are more people born spiritually each day than physically.

Following is a four-point outline explaining how you can come to know God. It is reprinted from a booklet entitled **Four Spiritual Laws.**

LAW ONE: God LOVES you, and offers a wonderful PLAN for your life.

God's Love: "For God so loved the world, that He gave His only begotten Son, that whoever believes in Him should not perish, but have eternal life" (John 3:16). *

* (References contained in this booklet should be read in context from the Bible wherever possible.)

God's Plan: (Christ speaking) "I came that they might have life, and might have it abundantly" (that it might be full and meaningful) (John 10:10).

Why is it that most people are not experiencing the abundant life?

Because...

LAW TWO: Man is SINFUL and SEPARATED from God. Therefore, He cannot know and experience God's love and plan for His life.

Man is Sinful: "For all have sinned and fall short of the glory of God" (Romans 3:23).

Man was created to have fellowship with God; but, because of his stubborn self-will, he chose to go his own independent way and fellowship with God was broken. This self-will, characterized by an attitude of active rebellion or passive indifference, is evidence of what the Bible calls sin.

Man is separated: "For the wages of sin is death" (spiritual separation from God) (Romans 6:23).

This diagram illustrates that God is holy and man is sinful. A great gulf separates the two. The arrows illustrate that man is continually trying to reach God and the abundant life through his own efforts, such as a good life, philosophy or religion.

HOLY GOD

SINFUL MAN

The third law explains the only way to bridge this gulf...

LAW THREE: Jesus Christ is God's ONLY provision for man's sin. Through Him you can know and experience God's love and plan for your life.

He died in our place: "But God demonstrates His own love toward us, in that while we were yet sinners, Christ died for us" (Romans 5:8).

He rose from the dead: "Christ died for our sins...He was buried...He was raised on the third day, according to the Scriptures...He appeared to Peter, then to the twelve. After that He appeared to more than five hundred..." (1 Corinthians 15:3-6).

He is the Only Way to God: "Jesus said to him, 'I am the way, and the truth, and the life; no one comes to the Father, but through Me' " (John 14:6).

This diagram illustrates that God has bridged the gulf which separates us from Him by sending His Son, Jesus Christ, to die on the cross in our place to pay the penalty for our sins.

It is not enough just to know these three laws...

LAW FOUR: We must individually RECEIVE Jesus Christ as Savior and Lord; then we can know and experience God's love and plan for our lives.

We must receive Christ: "But as many as received Him, to them He gave the right to become children of God, even to those who believe in His name" (John 1:12).

We receive Christ through faith: "For by grace you have been saved through faith; and that not of yourselves, it is the gift of God; not as a result of works, that no one should boast" (Ephesians 2:8,9).

When we receive Christ, we experience a new birth. (Read John 3:1-8.)

We receive Christ by personal invitation: (Christ is speaking): "Behold, I stand at the door and knock; if any one hears My voice and opens the door, I will come in to him" (Revelation 3:20).

Receiving Christ involves turning to God from self (repentance) and trusting Christ to come into our lives to forgive our sins and to make us the kind of people He wants us to be. Just to agree intellectually that Jesus Christ is The Son of God and that He died on the cross for our sins is not enough. Nor is it enough to have an emotional experience. We receive Jesus Christ by faith, as an act of the will.

These two circles represent two kinds of people:

SELF-DIRECTED LIFE
S — Self is on the throne
† — Christ is outside the life
● — Interests are directed
by self, often resulting in
discord and frustration

CHRIST-DIRECTED LIFE
† — Christ is in the life
and on the throne
S — Self is yielding to Christ
● — Interests are directed
by Christ, resulting in
harmony with God's plan

Which circle best represents your life?
Which circle would you like to have represent your life?

The following explains how you can receive Christ:

You can receive Christ right now by faith through prayer: (Prayer is talking with God.) God knows your heart and is not so concerned with your words as He is with the attitude of your heart. The following is a suggested prayer:

"Lord Jesus, I need You. Thank You for dying on the cross for my sins. I open the door of my life and receive You as my Savior and Lord. Thank you for forgiving my sins and giving me eternal life. Take control of the throne of my life. Make me the kind of person You want me to be."

Does this prayer express the desire of your heart? If it does, pray this prayer right now, and Christ will come into your life, as He promised.

How to know that Christ is in your life: Did you receive Christ into your life? According to His promise in Revelation 3:20, where is Christ right now in relation to you? Christ said that He would come into your life. Would He mislead you? On what authority do you know that God has answered your prayer? (The trustworthiness of God Himself and His Word.)

The Bible promises eternal life to all who receive Christ: "And the witness is this, that God has given us eternal life, and this life is in His Son. He who has the Son has the life; he who does not have the Son of God does not have the life. These things I have written to you who believe in the name of the Son of God, in order that you may know that you have eternal life" (1 John 5:11-13).

Thank God often that Christ is in your life and that He will never leave you (Hebrews 13:5). You can know on the basis of His promise that Christ lives in you and that you have eternal life, from the very moment you invite Him in. He will not deceive you.

Do not depend upon feelings: The promise of God's Word, the Bible—not our feelings—is our authority. The Christian lives by faith (trust) in the trustworthiness of God Himself and His Word. This train diagram illustrates the relationship between **fact** (God and His Word), **faith** (our trust in God and His Word), and **feeling** (the result of our faith and obedience) (John 14:21).

The train will run with or without the caboose. However, it would be useless to attempt to pull the train by the caboose. In the same way, we, as Christians, do not depend on feelings or emotions, but we place our faith (trust) in the trustworthiness of God and the promises of His Word.

Send to: Campus Crusade for Christ, P.O. Box 368, Abbotsford, B.C. V2S 4N9

MY RESPONSE...

☐ I have recently received Jesus Christ as my Lord and Savior.

☐ I am a Christian and I would like further help in getting to know Christ better.

☐ I am thinking seriously about becoming a Christian; please send me further information.

Name _____

Address _____

City _____

Province _____ Postal Code _____

Campus Crusade for Christ publishes other material which you may find helpful.

1. The Transferable Concepts: A set of nine booklets giving a practical guide to some important areas of the Christian life.

2. Ten Basic Steps Toward Christian Maturity: A series of Bible study booklets, each covering a different aspect of the Christian life.

(please turn over)

3. Evidence That Demands a Verdict: A 400-page volume of detailed, factual evidence for the historical reliability of the Christian faith.

Campus Crusade for Christ also offers conferences which provide training in how to live the Christian life and share your faith with others.

Further details of conferences and a full list of publications may be obtained by writing: Campus Crusade for Christ of Canada, Box 368, Abbotsford, B.C. V2S 4N9.

About the Author

Jim Talentino, M.Div. (cand.), B.Sc., B.Ed., played and coached Ontario Hockey Association Junior "A" hockey, attended Ithaca College, New York, on a hockey scholarship and had a brief professional try-out with the Detroit Red Wings of the NHL. After a number of years as a physical education teacher at a private boy's school, and as an administrator for the Team Canada Hockey College, he is now attending Canadian Theological College in Regina, Saskatchewan, in preparation for the ministry.